International Commodity Market Arrangements

IT IS WIDELY believed that primary commodities in international trade experience a higher degree of instability and a deteriorating long-term price trend in comparison with manufactured goods. To improve the stability of commodity markets and to increase the earnings of commodity producers, several international commodity agreements have been brought into operation. An intensive discussion has been taking place throughout on the alternative method of compensatory finance for achieving the aim of stability, possibly combined with built-in measures for the expansion of exporters' revenue.

This book provides an up-to-date survey of the working and effects of the tools used in various commodity agreements, and discusses the implications of compensatory finance, against a factual description of the operation of recent commodity agreements. As the measures analyzed are predominantly used to decrease the social and economic difficulties of underdeveloped countries, the emphasis is on the problems of those countries.

In the first chapter, the commodity market problems, which have initiated international action, are defined and discussed. Chapter 2 is devoted to underdeveloped countries, whose specific difficulties emanate from the high commodity concentration in their exports, which makes them dependent on conditions in commodity markets, and the inflexibilities in their economies, which prevent smooth adaptation to the changing commodity market conditions. Chapter 3 surveys the four commodity agreements established since 1945. Chapters 4–6 take up the different tools used in commodity agreements, while Chapter 7 analyzes the proposals for compensatory finance. Chapter 8, finally, discusses the empirical evidence of the effects of commodity instability, as it appears in some recent studies. The implications for future commodity stabilization measures, which emerge from these results, are also taken up.

Dr. Radetzki is a Ph.D. of the Stockholm School of Economics. He worked in 1961–68 with Kooperativa Forbundet, the Swedish Cooperative Union and Wholesale Society, spending four of these years as director of ICA Education Centre, a cooperative leadership training institution for South and East Asia, situated in New Delhi, and financed by Kooperativa Forbundet.

MARIAN RADETZKI

International Commodity Market Arrangements

A Study of the Effects of Post-War Commodity Agreements and Compensatory Finance Schemes

LONDON

C. HURST & CO.

First published by C. Hurst & Co.
40a Royal Hill, Greenwich, London S.E.10, England

SBN 90096625 4

Typesetting by Expedite Multiprint Ltd, London

Printed in Great Britain by
Billing & Sons Ltd, Guildford, England

FOREWORD

This study forms part of the varied research activities of the
Stockholm School of Economics. More and more attention is given
by economists to the problems of underdeveloped countries. The
present work seeks to scrutinize two methods frequently advocated
by those who recommend or decide on the aid and development
policies to be followed. It is my hope that the findings and conclusions will be of some use for the decision-makers of today as well
as for students of international economics, who will take over the
responsibilities tomorrow.

I am grateful for the permissions to quote from J. Pincus, <u>Trade,
Aid and Development</u> (McGraw-Hill), from Alasdair MacBean's
<u>Export Instability and Economic Development</u> (George Allen & Unwin;
Harvard University Press), from H. Johnson's <u>Economic Policies
towards Less Developed Countries</u> (Brookings), from an article by
R. H. Snape and B. S. Yamey in <u>Oxford Economic Papers</u> of July 1963,
and from various UNCTAD documents.

My sincere thanks are due to Professors Erik Dahmén, Assar
Lindbeck and Erik Lundberg for their guidance and valuable suggestions, and also to the Torsten and Ragnar Söderberg Foundations,
whose generous grant enabled me to undertake the work.

M. R.

October 1969

CONTENTS

I THE PROBLEM DEFINED

I.1 Purpose of study

It is a widely held belief that primary commodities (henceforth
referred to simply as "commodities") in international trade experience a higher degree of instability and a deteriorating long-term
price trend in comparison with manufactured goods. To improve
the stability of commodity markets and to increase the earnings of
commodity producers, several international commodity agreements
have been brought into operation. All along, an intensive discussion has been taking place on the alternative method of compensatory
finance, whereby the aim of stability, possibly combined with
built-in measures for the expansion of exporters' revenue, could
be achieved.

The purpose of this study is to scrutinize the working and effects of
the tools used in various commodity agreements, and to discuss the
implications of compensatory finance, against a factual description
of the operation of recent commodity agreements. As the measures
analyzed here are predominantly used to decrease the social and
economic hardships experienced by underdeveloped economies, the
emphasis of the study will be on the problems of u-countries
(u stands for underdeveloped, i for industrialized).

In this introductory chapter we will define and discuss the commodity market problems, which have initiated international action.
Chapter II is devoted to u-countries. Their specific difficulties
emanate from two factors. First, many u-countries have a high
commodity concentration in their exports, and this makes them
very dependent on the conditions in commodity markets. Second,
underdeveloped economies are characterized by rigidities and
inflexibilities, which prevent smooth adaptations to the changing
commodity market conditions. Chapter III will give a survey of
the four commodity agreements which have been established since
1945.

In chapters IV - VI we will take up the different tools used in
commodity agreements, while chapter VII analyzes the proposals
for compensatory finance. Chapter VIII, finally, discusses the
empirical evidence of the effects of commodity instability, as it
appears in some recent studies. The implications for future
commodity stabilization measures, emerging from these results,
will also be taken up in that chapter.

I.2 Economic and political considerations behind commodity market arrangements

The two problems which commodity arrangements try to solve are
unstable export prices and proceeds on the one hand, and excessively low or declining prices and proceeds on the other.

The difficulties experienced by commodity exporting countries,
which result from commodity instability, will be taken up in greater
detail in the next chapter. A mere enumeration of the most important ones will be given here. The exporting country will find it
difficult to carry through long-term economic development plans
which require stable and substantial foreign exchange resources,
if the export revenue fluctuates according to an unpredictable
pattern. It will be difficult to determine the optimal amount of
resources in the production of a commodity, if its prices experience sharp and frequent irregular fluctuations. Producer income
variations can cause severe social hardship, in particular when
production is carried on in small units. The inflexible structure
of underdeveloped economies will cause unemployment of resources,
if as a result of temporarily low prices, a production contraction
takes place.

On the importing side too, commodity instability is likely to create
problems. First, instability in commodity prices will complicate
investment planning for manufacturers. Where the commodity
input constitutes a substantial share of the total production cost, a
temporary increase in the price of the commodity may result in a
loss to the manufacturer if he feels that he cannot change his
product price too frequently, because a given price has been adver-
tised in his marketing activities. Assured supply and a high level
of price stability would be preferred by such manufacturers.
Where the imports of a commodity constitute a large share of total
imports, and the demand price elasticity is low, price volatility
will also cause undesirable instability in the country's balance of
payments.

Commodity concentration in exports is usually much higher than in imports. [1] In view of this, stabilization is likely to be more important to the exporting side. Nevertheless, the arguments presented above suggest that both parties have cause to be interested in and to promote short-term stabilization measures.

With regard to price-raising commodity arrangements, it may be interesting to note that in the late 1940's when, against the background of war scarcities, the discussion on commodity agreements was initiated, an important problem seemed to be that of excessive prices, and the Havana Charter stressed the significance of giving equal voting power to the consuming side in any international agreement to be established. Since the Korean War, few severe commodity scarcities have been experienced. The importing interests have therefore not been so keenly interested in the establishment of price-fixing agreements, and have been unwilling to pay the costs for their maintenance. The exporting side has been the most eager to regulate the markets.

The producing side has an obvious interest in price-raising measures as long as the marginal costs exceed marginal revenue. Between the two world wars, quite a number of agreements aiming at higher prices were reached between producers, and were opposed, sometimes quite forcefully, by the consuming interests. In the post-war period, the attitude of the importing countries has undergone an important change. Commodity production and exports weigh heaviest in the economies of u-countries. With the increasing interest in development assistance, the raising of commodity prices to levels above the unregulated market equilibrium has received the support of important i-countries because it has been regarded as an assistance measure whereby the lot of small individual producers can be improved, while the increase in exchange earnings is expected to promote the development efforts of the commodity-producing u-countries. A further argument frequently used in support of price-raising schemes has been the allegedly deteriorating terms of trade trend of commodities versus manufactured goods. We will return to this point in section I.5.

The support of i-countries for the maintenance of commodity prices at predetermined levels has not been purely altruistic in character. Price-increasing commodity arrangements as a rule also imply price stability over a period. As mentioned earlier,

4

this facilitates production and investment planning in i-countries.
The manufacturer in the importing country is likely to be more
interested in stable prices than in low prices. As long as all his
competitors are equally treated, the cost increase due to high
commodity prices can be shifted on to the consumer. In the long
run, of course, substitution in consumption and in manufacturing
can become a problem.

There has been frequently a political undertone in the price-raising
commodity market arrangements. In the case of the coffee agreement, for instance, the more or less openly proclaimed aim has
been to provide Latin America with higher exchange earnings and
thereby minimize the risks of social subversion and the introduction of non-capitalist political systems in the countries concerned.

There has been a persistent lack of emphasis in the price-raising
arrangements on the need for conformity between long period
trends of costs, prices and producer incomes. Reliance has been
placed on the equal representation of the importing and exporting
side, to keep the deviation of prices from market equilibrium at a
tenable level. It may be doubted whether such equal representation
is a sufficient measure to achieve this aim.

I.3   What do we mean by stabilization?

Definitions of instability

Commodity instability can be defined in a number of different ways.
In the context of this study, we are concerned with fluctuations of
any one of three magnitudes. Instability can thus be measured by
the variation of prices, by the changes in the volume of trade, or
by the fluctuations in the revenue received from the sales of a
commodity.

Ordinarily, instability measurements are concerned with annual
aggregates. This incorporates a bias in favor of stability, because
annual data will not fully reflect the seasonal or other brief fluctuations of the values studied.

The simplest way to measure instability is to consider year-to-
year percentage changes in the variables concerned. This is an
acceptable measurement, where the variable does not show any
trend development. On the other hand, if for instance the magni-

tude studied increases over the years at a fast and steady rate, year-to-year comparisons would indicate a high degree of "fluctuations", while in effect there had been no fluctuations at all. (Suppose that a variable develops along the series 100, 105, 110, 115, ... By measuring year-to-year changes, we get an instability of about 5% per year, in spite of the fact that the series represents a straight line in an ordinary graph. By correcting for trend, therefore, we will get no instability at all.) In a study of export price instability during the period 1948-58, Michaely uses the simple instability measure of year-to-year percentage changes, after concluding that no particular trend in price movements can be discerned. [2]

Correction for trend in the measurement of instability can be undertaken by various procedures. Most techniques assume a linear time trend. Sometimes the trend is conceived in the form of equal yearly percentage changes. In a semi-logarithmic diagram this will appear as a straight line. Instability will be measured as a percentage deviation of the magnitude concerned from the trend value for a particular year. Alternatively, instability can be estimated as the average percentage deviation from a five- or seven-year moving average, centered on the mid-year.

Commodity instability can be computed in the form of international aggregates. In this study, more interest will be attached to instability measurements for individual countries. In some cases attention is focused on the instability of total exports of a particular country, rather than of that country's exports of a specific commodity. An average of the instabilities of all exported goods has then to be calculated, each item being weighed against its importance in total exports.

Instability in any of the three variables specified above is the result of some shift of the demand or supply schedule, or both. Stabilization schemes are commonly established to moderate either price or revenue fluctuations. As a rule this is achieved by neutralizing the demand or supply shifts which have caused the instability in these variables to occur.

Price stabilization

A matter causing some difficulty in international price stabilization schemes is the selection of prices to be stabilized. There is some-

6

times a considerable difference between the variation in prices
received by producers, and those quoted in international markets.
Export tax cum subsidy programs can, for instance, shield the
individual producers from the international markets, and the
inconvenience of unstable prices is shifted in this way from producers to their governments. In view of the ability of the governments to make adjustments in the internal price system, the prices
considered in international stabilization schemes are usually those
quoted in international trade.

Stabilization schemes can have the objective of reducing the nominal
price movements. Alternatively their purpose may be to stabilize
the commodity's price in relation to other goods. Even in this
case several differing definitions can be conceived. Commodity
prices can be stabilized in terms of the goods which producers buy,
in terms of some general cost-of-living index, or simply in terms
of the total imports of the country concerned.

In practice international stabilization has as a rule concerned the
nominal price. The probable reason for this is the extreme intri-
cacies involved in determining and keeping track of a commodity's
relative price.

Stabilization of prices will often have the effect of destabilizing
revenue. Only in some special cases, for instance where a stable
supply function cuts varying and inelastic demand functions, will
price stabilization have an evening effect on revenue. This is
illustrated in Fig. I. 1A, where due to periodic shifts in the demand
schedule, price varies between P_1 and P_3, while revenue fluctuates
from P_1Q_2 to P_3Q_3. Stabilization of prices at P_E will render
revenue fluctuations between P_EQ_1 and P_EQ_4, which are smaller
than with unstable prices. This may be a correct description of the
market situation for some price insensitive non-agricultural raw
materials whose supply is unaffected by weather vagaries, strikes
etc. In most other cases, e.g. where the variable demand is
price elastic (Fig. I. 1B), or where supply varies (Fig. I. 1C), price
stabilization will in fact have a destabilizing effect on revenue.
A correlation of 45 country indices of instability of export revenue
and price shows no significant value,[3] which seems to support
the above point that revenue stability is not usually dependent on
price stabilization.

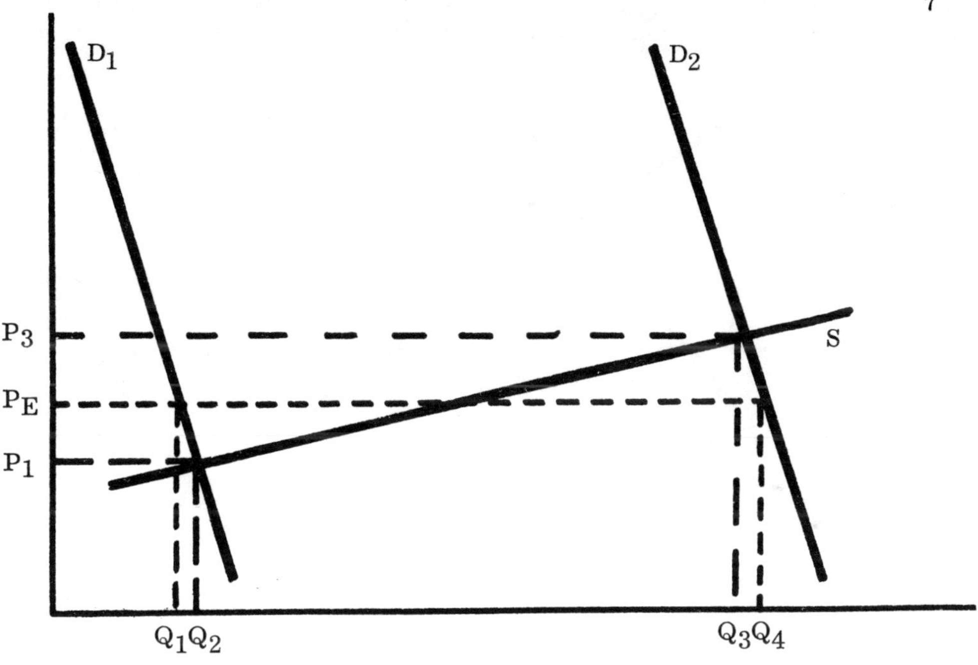

Fig. I. 1A
$$\frac{P_E Q_4}{P_E Q_1} < \frac{P_3 Q_3}{P_1 Q_2}$$

which proves that price stabilization will stabilize revenue in this case.

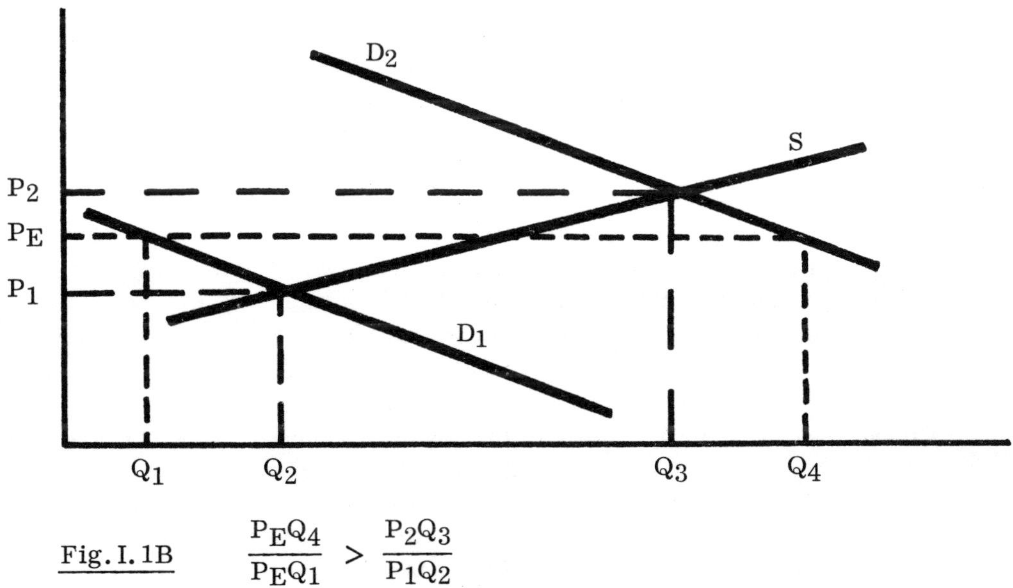

Fig. I. 1B
$$\frac{P_E Q_4}{P_E Q_1} > \frac{P_2 Q_3}{P_1 Q_2}$$

which proves that price stabilization will destabilize revenue in this case.

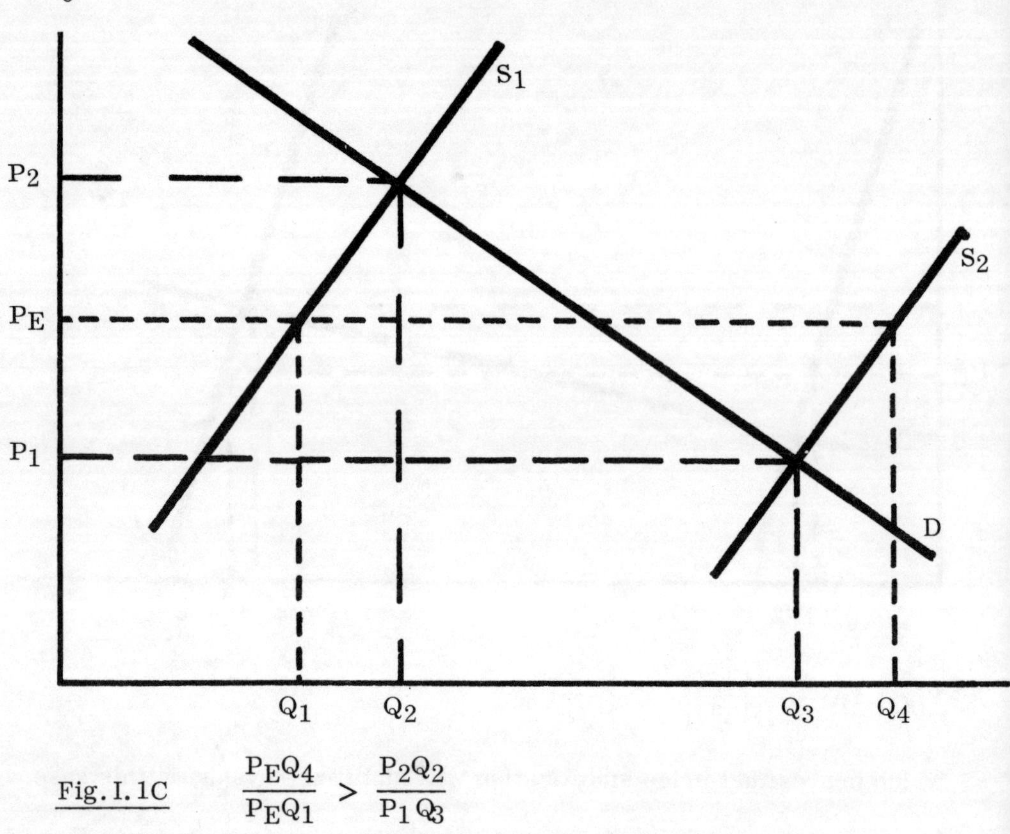

$$\text{Fig. I. 1C} \qquad \frac{P_E Q_4}{P_E Q_1} > \frac{P_2 Q_2}{P_1 Q_3}$$

which proves that price stabilization will destabilize revenue in this case.

Stabilization of revenue

Commodity producers or commodity exporting countries will often
be more interested in stabilization of export revenue than in price
stability. Some stabilization schemes have consequently the objective to stabilize export revenue without regard to what happens with
prices.

A conceptual difficulty similar to that discussed under price stabilization is experienced here as well. Revenue stabilization can be
defined in a number of ways. One definition involves stabilization
in nominal terms. We have in this case the further choice of
stabilizing revenue in terms of the national currency, or in terms
of an international reserve currency unit. Alternatively one can
conceive revenue stabilization relative to other magnitudes, e.g.

in terms of the country's import capacity. The definitional and estimating problems appear to be still more intricate than in the case of relative price determination. In practice, therefore, revenue stabilization schemes ordinarily have the objective of stabilizing the export proceeds in terms of their dollar value.

Another problem in revenue stabilization emerges from a conscious decision by a country to cut its export supply. Ordinarily, the purpose of international revenue stabilizing schemes is to protect commodity exporters from unexpected revenue changes. But changes in exports can be the result of internal policy measures, for instance when the producers decide to reduce export supply in order to consume more, or to transfer production to a different commodity, and thereby cause the export proceeds to fall. The question then arises whether such types of instability also warrant international neutralization. If the decision is against international action to rectify deliberately induced instability, then discretionary measures will be required, which enable the administrators of the scheme to look into the reasons for supply variations.

A policy choice has to be made between stabilization of revenue from exports of specific commodities, and alternatively from the total export proceeds of the country concerned. In very few countries are the exports dominated by only one commodity. For countries other than those few, specific commodity revenue stabilization programs are probably of less interest than total export revenue stabilization. If in Malaysia, a typical two-commodity exporter, rubber revenue falls while tin proceeds increase, so that total export revenue remains constant, the problem of instability will be somewhat easier to tackle internally, for instance by a variable export tax program, than when total export proceeds fluctuate. Recent stabilization efforts have also tended to concern themselves more with total export revenue stabilization.

Stabilization and trend

It was indicated above that instability is generally measured as the year-to-year variations from a trend. The trend is based on the actual outcome over several past years. A scheme neutralizing all instability will cause the year-to-year values of the variable concerned to conform with the trend. Successful stabilization measures will therefore perpetuate the trend line.

B

Suppose, however, that market conditions change and that in the absence of stabilization measures, the trend line would gradually assume a new and different shape from what it had been before. If stabilization along the original trend is successfully maintained, there will be no opportunity to notice the change which has occurred. Stabilization will therefore be maintained at levels which are gradually removed from the unregulated market equilibrium. There is a likelihood that the tensions which this ever-increasing discrepancy creates will eventually break the whole stabilization arrangement.

The problem identified here, i.e. the risk of losing track of the unregulated market equilibrium trend, is more or less inherent in all the tools used in the post-war commodity agreements. It is largely avoided, on the other hand, in the general compensatory finance schemes, where commodity markets are not directly affected by the stabilization measures.

I.4   Causes to and evidence of commodity instability

The mechanism

Following Walras' excess demand hypothesis, we will assume a very simple price reaction mechanism. Starting from a price level given by the intersection of the demand and supply schedules, the price will rise if there is a positive shift in the demand schedule, or a negative one in the supply schedule. The price will decline, if the opposite demand or supply shifts occur. Price instability is estimated from yearly price changes. The demand and supply schedules considered are therefore short-term ones, and show the possible adjustments which can take place within this period, in order to reach a temporary equilibrium. The ultimate price change will depend on the size of the shift as well as on the price elasticities of the schedules. Other things being equal, the lower the elasticity, the sharper the price swing. To provide an explanation of commodity price instability, we must therefore look into both the price elasticities and the shifts in demand and supply.

The price reaction pattern becomes much more complicated, if there is a lag in the adjustment of supply or demand to a changed price. Under such conditions, explosive cobweb patterns can sometimes develop, and price will not automatically reach an equilibrium level. An example of such a development is given in Chapter VI.

Changes in export revenue are similarly caused by shifts in the
demand and supply schedules in a country's exports. With a shift
in the supply schedule, price and quantity will move in opposite
directions, and revenue will be relatively more stable than prices.
With demand variations, price and quantity move in the same
direction, and revenue will be less stable than prices.

Price elasticities

Price elasticities are very difficult to determine. The scarce
estimates which are available measure as a rule the short-term
interrelation between price and quantity.

Supply elasticities vary with the commodity. For one-year crops,
the price elasticity of supply is low in the very short run, but may
be quite high if a period including a full crop season is considered.
Where production increase requires heavy investment over several
years, the price elasticity of supply is low from one year to the
next, but considerable if the price change is maintained for longer.
In the short run, the production responses to a price rise for such
commodities will primarily depend on the possibility to use more
intensively the existing capital stock. Rubber trees can be tapped
harder, tea leaves plucked more frequently, while overtime or
additional shifts can be introduced in mineral extraction activities.
In distinction from production elasticity, supply elasticity is higher
for commodities where producers and speculators operate stocks.
An increase in prices will then ordinarily induce stock sales,
whereby supply is increased. (Note however the result of stock-
holders' expectations that further price increases will follow.
Supply from stocks will then decrease, and may even become
negative, as speculators buy to increase their holdings.)

Price elasticities of demand vary between commodities and
markets. For commodities without close substitutes, demand
elasticities are usually low.

An estimate for coffee and lead renders short-run values below
0.5. [4) Where substitutes are available, e.g. for natural rubber
or cotton, the demand elasticity must be considerably higher.
Tropical commodities, which are still considered a luxury in the
poorer countries, will have a higher demand elasticity there than
when they are marketed in rich countries, where their consumption
is high and established. Where processing or manufacturing costs

are high, the price of the final consumer product may be only mar-
ginally dependent on the price of the commodity. Commodity price
variations will in such cases have a very limited effect on the final
demand from consumers. The result of this is a high degree of
demand insensitivity to price changes in the commodity. Strategic
needs will likewise create "demand at any price", with a price
elasticity close to zero.

Supply and demand changes

Various causes for changes in supply can be discerned. Agricultural commodities experience harvest variations. These may be
random as for wheat, or cyclical as for coffee and olives.
Strikes can sharply affect the supply conditions for minerals, the
extraction of which is more dependent on organized labor. Political disturbances may cut the supplies of all types of commodities.
Sabotage on a bridge of the copper road from Zambia to Dar-es-
Salaam, for instance, caused a perceptible copper price increase
on the London Metal Exchange. [5]

World demand for a commodity can also vary for a number of
reasons. Technical innovations can suddenly change the demand
for a commodity. Business cycles are another important cause
for variation in demand. Income increases will result in a higher
demand, at least for non-inferior goods. Some commodities are
affected by stock fluctuations, which can strongly destabilize
demand. Stock cycles may in their turn depend on speculative,
commercial or political reasons. After 1945, the USA established
huge strategic stocks of a number of commodities, predominantly
metals. Purchases for strategic stock-holding, or sales, if the
stocks are found to be superfluous, can create considerable market
disturbances.

International markets for agricultural commodities produced by
both u- and i-countries often experience a high degree of volatility.
This is because i-countries' domestic markets are isolated through
comprehensive national agricultural policies. The demand or
supply from i-countries, which often forms a sizable proportion of
international trade, will be a result of national adjustments of
short-term imbalances between domestic production and consumption, and will not be influenced by the world market price. A
typical example of such residual world markets is that for sugar.
Suppose that the harvest in i-countries is above average. With

prevailing agricultural regulations, the price on the domestic
i-markets is not allowed to fall. Domestic consumption will therefore not be increased, and the surplus thrown into the international
market will be larger than in the absence of protective agricultural
policies.

Low short-term price elasticities and a considerable variability in
demand and supply in many commodity markets provide an entirely
plausible argument for the belief that commodities experience a
high degree of instability. In a while we shall look at the factual
evidence.

The role of speculation on price instability

Speculation is possible only in standardized products, and is therefore much more common in commodity markets than in the markets
for manufactured goods. In principle, the presence of speculators
should diminish the price swings. Ordinarily, speculators will buy
if they feel that the price has fallen below equilibrium, thereby
preventing a further decrease in prices, and sell when they think
that prices are too high, so that their action stops prices from
undergoing further increases. Speculation may have a destabilizing
effect on the market, if the speculators' expectations are faulty.
Suppose that speculators buy on a price fall, in the belief that the
fall is temporary: if they are wrong, and the decrease in prices
is due to a permanent change in market conditions, the eventual
sales which speculators have to make, will temporarily drive the
prices below the level which would be reached in the absence of
speculation.

Speculation is highly facilitated and most common in markets where
speculators can work with future contracts. A market in future
deliveries relieves the speculator from the inconvenience and cost
of physical stock-holding. In the absence of a future market, the
speculator will have to acquire physical stocks of the commodity.
How much must the price fall below equilibrium level in the belief
of the speculator, before he starts buying? Suppose he expects
that he will have to keep his stock for one year. Financial and
stock-holding costs will then amount to at least 10%. It would be
difficult to imagine a risk and profit margin of less than 5%, and
probably this margin has to be set much higher. Thus we see that
in a commodity market without future contracts, price will ordinarily have to fall by much more than 15% below what is thought to
be equilibrium, before the speculators enter to buy.

14

<u>Some figures on commodity instability</u>

Table I.1 illustrates the wide difference between commodities in
the extent of their price and revenue instability. The figures,
being 10-year averages, hide yearly variations, which are much
higher. For cocoa, the extreme year-to-year percentage price
changes during the period have been +66 and -21, for rubber +56
and -26.[6] The instability in total value concerns aggregates of
both years and countries. This hides the individual year and
country variations, which are certainly higher than the aggregates.

Statistics for 39 commodities for the period 1950-61 indicate that
on an average, price and volume moved in the same direction in
seven of the eleven years.[7] Price and volume move in the same
direction, we may recall, if the change is mainly due to a shift in
demand. One could expect this figure to be higher for non-
agricultural commodities, which are not dependent on harvest
fluctuations. However, no marked difference can be noticed
between the agricultural and non-agricultural commodity classes.
Commodity price fluctuations therefore seem to be caused in
roughly equal measure by variations in supply and in demand.

What can be said about commodity instability in relation to the
instability of manufactured goods? Coppock and Michaely have
attempted some calculations. For the period 1948-58, Coppock's
export revenue instability index renders a higher value for manufactures than for commodities. In a finer division, and using the
logarithmic variance method, Coppock obtains the following
instability index figures for the value of world trade between the
years 1952 and 1957:[8]

1.	Food	5.1
2.	Agricultural raw materials	4.1
3.	Minerals	9.9
4.	Fuels	5.9
5.	Capital goods	6.1
6.	Consumer goods	4.6
7.	Other manufactures	6.6
8.	Base metals	10.5
9.	Total	4.4

Table I.1   Some primary commodities classified according to the degree of instability in world trade, 1953 - 64

Commodity	Instability index[*]	
	Unit value	Total value[**]
Black pepper	47.3	47.2
Tungsten	39.3	–
Cocoa beans	19.8	13.7
Manganese ore and concentrates	18.9	26.7
Raw jute	17.0	7.4
Natural rubber	16.3	17.0
Hard fibres	15.7	15.8
Lead	14.2	13.6
Zinc ore and concentrates	14.0	18.4
Coconut oil	13.8	15.9
Copper	13.7	13.3
Zinc	13.6	19.4
Jute goods	12.9	11.2
Sugar, raw	12.8	11.3
Coffee	12.0	7.5
Copra	12.0	8.2
Tin	9.5	19.9
Tea	8.5	7.0
Rice	8.3	9.0
Groundnut oil	7.5	11.3
Maize	7.4	18.3
Bauxite	5.6	7.2
Palm oil	5.5	5.5
Cotton	5.2	9.0
Groundnuts	5.1	8.4
Tobacco	3.1	4.3

[*] Instability has been measured by the coefficient of variation of residuals from a linear trend.

[**] Calculations of total value for certain commodities based on exports from underdeveloped countries, for others on total world exports.

Source: UNCTAD: Commodity problems and policies, TD/8/Suppl.1, 14 Nov. 1967, Stencil, p.16-17.

Michaely tries to measure the price instability of commodities versus manufactured goods, and for the years 1948-57 he gets an average percentage change from year to year of 6.4 for commodities against 5.7 for manufactures. [9]

The weakness with Coppock's and Michaely's figures is that they are so highly aggregated. The aggregates probably contain much higher fluctuations for individual products. They seem sufficient however, to refute the common belief that commodities are generally more unstable than manufactured goods. The crucial distinction with regard to instability is probably not that between commodities and manufactured goods, but rather between the variability of demand and supply and the short-run price elasticities for different products. These factors are likely to differ much more among various commodities than they do between commodities as a group and manufactured goods.

I.5   The case of deteriorating commodity terms of trade

At the outset it may be interesting to note the common view among economists in the beginning of this century that commodity terms of trade, e.g. the amount of manufactured goods obtainable for a given quantity of commodities, were likely to improve in course of time, in view of diminishing marginal returns in primary production and diminishing costs in manufacturing. [10]

Nowadays opinions have changed, and it is widely believed that the commodity terms of trade are declining. The evidence cited in support of this takes as a rule the Korean war boom as a base from which the trend is calculated. During the years of the boom, and particularly in 1951, commodity prices rose to an extreme level, from which it would be unrealistic to calculate any trends. This is clearly illustrated in Chart I.1.

For longer periods, meaningful terms of trade series are extremely difficult to construct, and the degree of uncertainty is high. [11] Older statistical data are not very reliable. By a deliberate selection of base year and time period studied, almost any result can be obtained. If the index starts with a period when commodity prices were high, it is very likely to show deteriorating relative commodity prices. A commodity terms of trade index must by definition be highly aggregated. Thus, generally declining relative commodity prices do not preclude the existence of commodities with rapidly rising prices. For policy decisions on specific commodities such an index will not take us far, and information will be required on the development of individual commodity prices.

The technical construction of the index is also crucial for the outcome. Various methods treat new products in different ways. Manufactured goods often experience a price fall soon after their introduction. A chain index will therefore tend to give too heavy weights to such products, with the result that the commodity terms of trade will improve. Fixed base indexes, on the other hand, may completely omit products introduced after the base year, and will consequently soon lose their actuality.

Commodities are standardized, and it is relatively easy to compare their prices over longer periods. Not so for manufactured goods, where we can suspect a gradual improvement in quality. Erik Lundberg provides an interesting example of electric generators and turbines in Sweden, whose price index increased by some 50% over a 15-year period. Simultaneously their quality improved so fast that their prices measured in "efficiency units" remained more or less constant. [12] If we could take proper note of such improvements in our statistical measurements, then the commodity terms of trade would be considerably improved.

The price indexes of most commodities are calculated in London or New York, and include transport costs. An index showing a decline of the commodity terms of trade could therefore simply reflect the very sizable cost decreases in transport, which have taken place over the past decades.

In view of all the reservations taken up above, it is not surprising that economists who have tried to calculate the long-term commodity terms of trade developments, have come to very differing results, from which conclusions about a long-term pattern are difficult to draw.

In Chart I.1, an attempt is made to illustrate the price developments of various groups of goods since 1948. What the chart shows is a price decrease of some 5% for commodities over this 18-year period, and a simultaneous increase of 9% in the price of manufactured goods. It seems that the relative price change, amounting to less than 1% per year over the period, is well within the margin of possible distortions in the index calculations, due to the problems

Chart I.1 **Price indices by commodity classes**

Base 1958 = 100   Yearly averages

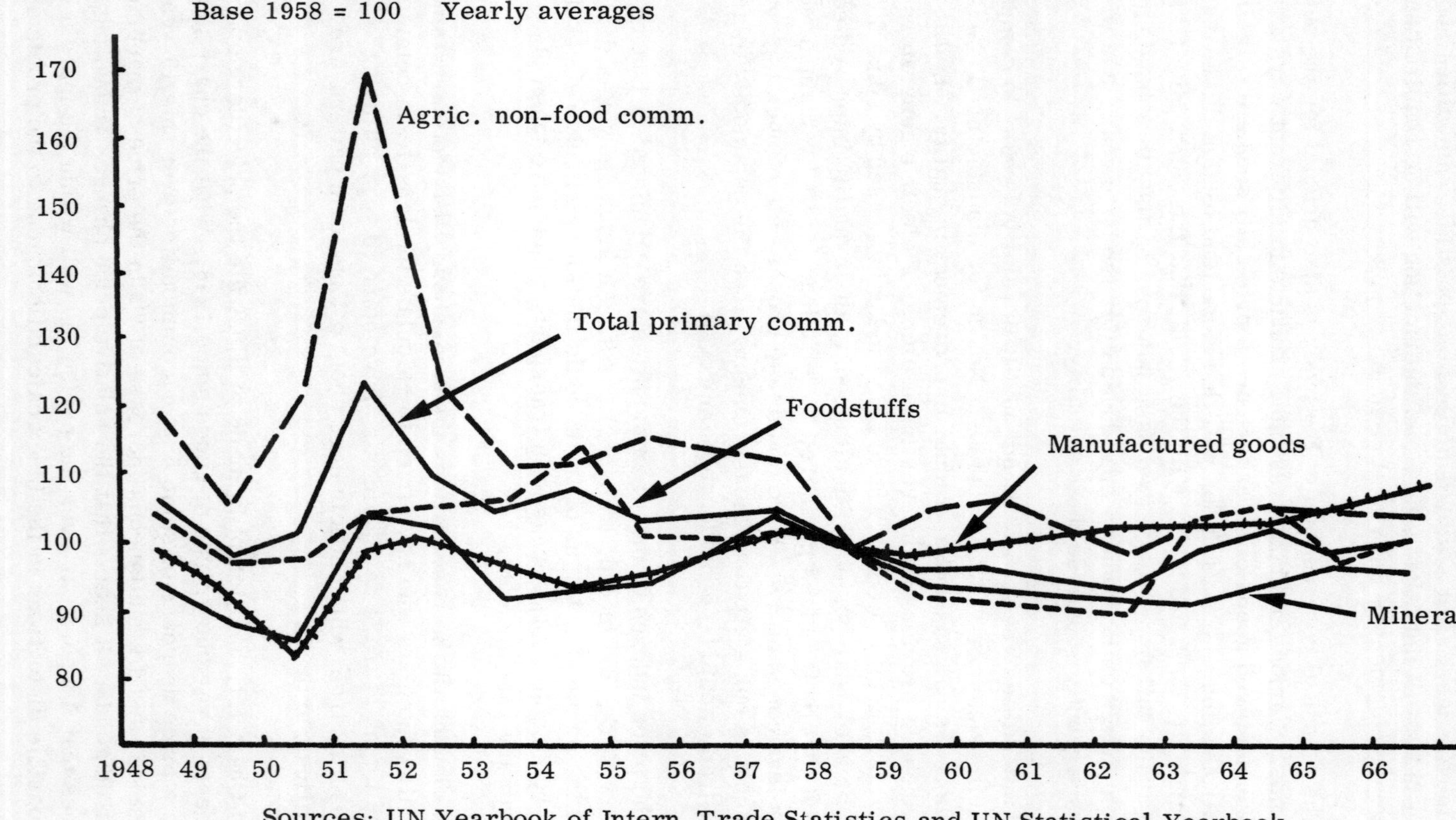

Sources: UN Yearbook of Intern. Trade Statistics and UN Statistical Yearbook

taken up above, and that therefore no definite deductions about the relative commodity prices can be made on the basis of these figures.

I.6   Alternative stabilization measures

International agreements based upon <u>export</u> or production <u>restrictions</u> have been widely used to adjust supply so as to protect the price level from temporary variations, or to keep it permanently above the unregulated market equilibrium.

<u>Multilateral contracts</u>, with significant importer obligations, are in the main a development occurring since 1945. For reasons which are often politically flavored, the importing countries agree to buy specific quantities of the commodity concerned at or above the established price. Producing countries frequently have to limit their exports to make a multilateral contract workable.

<u>Buffer stocks</u> have been mainly operated as a supplementary measure to export restriction schemes. With limited resources at their disposal, buffer stocks cannot serve for permanent price-raising purposes. They are on the other hand a flexible instrument to even out temporary price volatility.

<u>Compensatory finance schemes</u> are an outcome of the growing feeling that it is better to leave the commodity markets themselves unregulated, while assisting the producing countries to overcome the problems connected with instability or with declining commodity prices. A further development of compensatory finance schemes has emerged out of a recognition that general export instability is probably a larger problem to commodity-producing countries than the instability in one specific commodity only. The more recent compensatory finance scheme proposals have consequently the purpose to help in overcoming the overall national export revenue instability in u-countries.

Before we return to a more detailed discussion of the different commodity arrangement tools and their effects, we will take up in chapter II the problems encountered by those u-countries whose exports are highly commodity-concentrated, while chapter III will offer a factual description of the four commodity agreements which have been in operation in the post-war period.

Notes and references to Chapter I

1)   M. Michaely, <u>Concentration in International Trade</u>,
Amsterdam 1962, Ch. 2.

2)   M. Michaely, <u>Concentration in International Trade</u>,
Amsterdam 1962, pp. 66-67.

3)   A. MacBean, <u>Export Instability and Economic Development</u>,
London 1966, Ch. 2.

4)   UNCTAD: <u>Commodity problems and policies</u>, TD/8/Suppl. 1,
14 Nov. 1967, stencil, p. 60.

5)   Information from interview with Swedish Metal Wholesalers,
Söderberg & Haak.

6)   UNCTAD I, New York 1964, Proceedings, Vol. III, p. 109.

7)   Op. cit., p. 85.

8)   J. D. Coppock, <u>International Economic Instability</u>, New York,
1962, p. 41.

9)   M. Michaely, <u>Concentration in International Trade</u>,
Amsterdam 1962, p. 75.

10)   See for instance J. M. Keynes, 'Note on the return of estimated
value of foreign trade of the UK at the prices of 1900',
<u>Economic Journal</u> 1912

11)   For a fuller description of the problems in the terms of trade
index construction, see L. Nyberg & S. Viotti, <u>Terms of trade
mellan utvecklade länder och utvecklingsländer</u>,
Trebetygsuppsats, Handelshögskolan, Stockholm, June 1968.

12)   Erik Lundberg, <u>Problem omkring produktionsfunktionsanalysen</u>,
Stockholm, Feb. 1968, stencil, p. 21.

II U-COUNTRIES AND THE COMMODITY PROBLEMS

II.1 Role of commodities for u-countries

Commodities constitute between 50 and 60% of total world trade.
Although the share of u-countries in commodity exports only
amounts to some 35%, their export trade is highly dominated by
commodities. For 1959-61, FAO calculated that of total u-
country exports of $ 26.9 billion, 23.8 billion, or nearly 90%
consisted of commodities.[1]   Although exports of manufactures
from u-countries have grown at high rates, the dominant position
of commodities has not been substantially changed. About 80% of
internationally traded commodities are exported to i-countries.
Table II.1 provides a more detailed information on the most
important commodities with regard to trade and source of supply.

There exists a negative correlation between a country's development level and its commodity concentration in exports.[2]   The
more developed the country, the more diversified is its economy
likely to be, and the greater the number of different goods in its
exports. The highest commodity concentration is therefore found
among u-countries. In the following 13 countries, three commodities accounted for more than 80% of total export value in the years
1959-61.[3]

	%		%
Iraq	98	Ghana	84
Venezuela	98	New Zealand	84
Colombia	92	Rhodesia	82
Ivory Coast	91	Costa Rica	82
Ceylon	90	Sudan	81
Cuba	86	Uruguay	81
Argentina	86		

With the exception of New Zealand, all those countries belong to
the underdeveloped category. With such heavy concentration, one
or a few commodities become a very important source of exchange
earnings, employment, income, savings and investment.

Table II. 1

Primary commodities: Imports into industrial countries, [a]
1962

Order and commodity	Value of imports from [b] (millions of dollars)		
	All sources	Primary exporting countries [c]	Developing countries [d]
1 Petroleum, crude	5 736.0	5 316.8	5 316.8
2 Coffee	1 737.5	1 717.1	1 716.3
3 Petroleum and products	3 112.8	1 455.3	1 443.7
4 Copper	1 703.5	932.7	899.4
5 Sugar	1 139.4	1 001.8	885.6
6 Cotton	1 424.2	871.2	870.6
7 Rubber	1 011.5	764.1	763.9
8 Iron ore	1 414.7	709.9	695.1
9 Cocoa	516.2	443.7	440.2
10 Tea and maté	466.1	439.6	439.5
11 Wood, rough	795.0	399.0	391.8
12 Bananas	375.8	359.9	359.9
13 Wool	1 972.5	1 513.2	294.6
14 Wine	558.8	279.6	272.5
15 Oil-seed cake and meal	479.3	264.1	257.1
16 Tobacco	794.1	241.2	238.2
17 Meat, fresh, chilled, frozen	1 267.7	690.8	237.7
18 Tin	264.5	198.5	198.5
19 Ground-nuts	213.8	209.6	198.3
20 Bauxite	221.8	192.7	192.6
21 Maize	879.8	290.7	179.5
22 Oranges and tangerines	418.3	210.4	168.7
23 Copra	167.7	167.3	166.6
24 Hides and skins	521.8	285.6	158.1
25 Jute	161.4	157.4	157.4
26 Wheat	1 047.1	253.9	148.8
27 Fish	623.4	175.8	140.9
28 Phosphates, natural	188.5	121.6	121.6
29 Fish meal	180.0	140.0	117.0
30 Manganese ore	151.7	134.8	112.4
31- 140 All other items	16 975.3	3 744.7	2 729.1
TOTAL imports of primary commodities	46 520.2	23 683.0	20 312.4

Source: Bureau of General Economic Research and Policies of the United Nations Secretariat, based on data compiled by the Statistical Office of the United Nations.

[a] Belgium-Luxembourg, Canada, Denmark, France, Federal Republic of Germany, Iceland, Ireland, Italy, Japan, Netherlands, Norway, Portugal, Sweden, Switzerland, Turkey, United Kingdom, United States, plus Austria and Finland for 3-digit SITC items.

	Imports from primary exporting countries[b]	Imports from developing countries[d]		
			As percentage of all primary commodity imports from developing countries	
As percentage of imports of each commodity	Individual item as percentage of all primary commodity imports from the primary exporting countries	As percentage of imports of each commodity	Individual item	Cumulated
92.7	22.8	92.7	26.3	26.3
98.8	7.4	98.8	8.5	34.8
46.8	6.2	46.4	7.1	41.9
54.8	4.0	52.8	4.4	46.3
87.9	4.3	77.7	4.4	50.7
61.2	3.7	61.1	4.3	55.0
75.5	3.3	75.5	3.8	58.8
50.2	3.0	49.1	3.4	62.2
86.0	1.9	85.3	2.2	64.4
94.3	1.9	94.3	2.2	66.6
50.2	1.7	49.3	1.9	68.5
95.8	1.5	95.8	1.8	70.3
76.7	6.5	14.9	1.5	71.8
50.0	1.2	48.8	1.0	73.1
55.1	1.1	53.6	1.3	74.4
30.4	1.0	30.0	1.2	75.6
54.5	3.0	18.8	1.2	76.8
75.0	0.8	75.0	1.0	77.8
98.0	0.9	92.7	1.0	78.8
86.9	0.8	86.8	1.0	79.8
33.0	1.2	20.4	0.9	80.7
50.3	0.9	40.3	0.8	81.5
99.7	0.7	99.3	0.8	82.3
54.7	1.2	30.3	0.8	83.1
97.5	0.7	97.5	0.8	83.9
24.2	1.1	14.2	0.7	84.6
28.2	0.8	22.6	0.7	85.3
64.5	0.5	64.5	0.6	85.9
77.8	0.6	65.0	0.6	86.5
88.9	0.6	74.1	0.6	87.1
22.1	15.8	16.1	13.0	100.0
51.1	100.0	43.8	100.0	100.0

[b] Measured f.o.b. for Canada and the United States, and c.i.f. for all other importing countries.

[c] Latin America, Caribbean, Islands, Africa, West Asia (other than Turkey), southern and south-eastern Asia, Oceania.

[d] Primary exporting countries less Australia, New Zealand and South Africa.

From: UNCTAD I, UN New York 1964, Proceedings, Vol. III, p. 12.

24

The significance of commodities in the economies of many u-
countries has resulted in a considerable public involvement in
commodity production and trade. This government influence has
taken a multiplicity of forms.

Taxation of commodity exports is very common. It is difficult to
apply general income or profit taxes in u-countries. In the early
stages of economic development, external trade provides the best
facilities to tax.[4)] As the major share of u-countries' exports
consists of commodities, a substantial proportion of government
revenue will be dependent on the commodity sector.

A further step to public control over commodities is the establishment of national marketing boards, to which all producers are
forced to sell. Export marketing now becomes the sole responsibility of this government agency, and the internal producer prices
can be completely separated from those obtained in the international
market. Organizations of this type are functioning in many African
and Asian countries. Their activities can include a number of
functions in addition to internal purchases and export sales. In
many cases they improve grading and packaging practices, supply
superior seeds, and provide extension services of various kinds to
the individual producers.[5)] As a final step to full control of the
commodity sector, the government may choose to nationalize.
This is what has happened to tin in Bolivia and copper in the Congo
(Kinshasa).

A consequence of the increasing governmental intervention in
commodity markets is that the supply side will become gradually
more oligopolistic in character. While individual producers can
generally sell all their output at the market-determined price, the
price determination in markets, where governments control the
supply side, will depend more on bargaining strength and skill, and
on existing collusion on the producing or consuming side. Some
commodity markets, like for instance that for copper, have of
course long had an oligopolistic character, in view of the small
number of producing enterprises.

II.2 Effects of instability

Quite a number of u-countries, whose economies are concentrated
on unstable commodities, experience a considerable price and
revenue instability in their exports. The difficulties which they

experience will probably be greater than those of a corresponding
export instability in more developed economies. The principal
reason for this is that a developed country, with a more diversified
and flexible economy, will have better facilities for effective
countercyclical monetary and fiscal policies, whereby to counter
the shocks from the export sector. If, in addition, the commodity
price trend is declining, it will be still more difficult for a u-
country, depending on such commodity exports, to maintain internal
stability, while carrying on a development program, which is likely
to require substantial amounts of foreign exchange.

Of course, price changes are not bad per se. They are the signals
to increase or reduce production of a commodity. The question is
whether the signals are reliable, and not excessively strong in
relation to the desirable effect which they should have on resource
allocation. There is almost general agreement that the short-run
price variations in commodity markets are often a misleading or
extreme guide for resource allocation purposes, and that therefore
it seems desirable to counteract them by market regulation.[6]

Two diverging views have been brought forward. It has been
argued that the export revenue instability experienced by commodity-
producing countries could be beneficial to their economic development, because more capital can be formed when incomes and
exporters' profits are high only periodically.[7] This notion is
derived from the permanent income hypothesis, according to which
consumption is based on the assured permanent income, while a
major share of the additional transitory income is saved and
becomes available for investment purposes. It has also been
claimed that to even out commodity price fluctuations would be
disadvantageous, because it would remove the incentives to reallocate resources.[8] In the context of the export instability
experienced by u-countries, these views do not seem convincing.

First, with regard to investment and instability, it could well be
the other way round, e.g. that a higher living standard is established during the export boom. This will then cut into savings when
income falls again, and so lead to lower total savings over the cycle.
Furthermore, during the export boom the resources which can be
used for expansion of capacity in export production are already
fully employed, and it would be difficult to transform additional
savings into an expansion of the capital stock. The high export
profits, on the other hand, make a redirection of investment into
other fields improbable.

C

The role of price instability in improving allocative efficiency is also doubtful. In an underdeveloped economy a substantial proportion of the population is employed in subsistence agriculture, on which market price changes have limited effects. Very often such an economy contains a considerable open or hidden unemployment. This results to some extent from distorted wage levels. Due to the prevailing social structure, wages in the agricultural sector are equal to the average rather than the marginal product of labor. To attract labor, industry must pay wages which are at least equal to those offered in agriculture. The resulting wage level in industry is higher than it would have been if agricultural wages corresponded to the marginal product of labor, and industrial employment is consequently smaller. In part, unemployment also reflects the inflexibility of the economy. Lack of capital in general and of foreign exchange in particular prevents the domestic sectors from expanding and increasing their use of labor, when export income falls. This inflexibility is accentuated by other bottlenecks and rigidities, like scarcity of managerial talent, immobility of labor, illiteracy, inability to break with development-hampering traditions, and a general lack of information about employment and profit opportunities.[9] In such conditions, export price instability will at most confuse the situation. Rather than inducing reallocation of productive resources, a temporary price fall is likely to lead to reduction of production and employment in the export sector without increased employment opportunities elsewhere. We should note, however, that the problem of efficient resource allocation is usually not simplified by international commodity agreements. If the tools which are used to regulate the market fix the price at a predetermined level, then prices will be of no help as a guide to rational allocation decisions.

Where the commodity is produced by a large class of small-scale farmers, a price decrease resulting from diminished demand could alternatively lead to unchanged production, but at the same time a fall in the earnings of producers. This is what will probably happen if the farmers have no ready alternative use for their land, or when the land is planted with tree crops, e.g. coconut or rubber, which it would be unwise to cut due to a temporary price fluctuation. A price fall could bring the farmers' earnings below subsistence, with severe social consequences. The situation is further aggravated by the undeveloped social security and relief programs in most u-countries.

Taxation of commodity producers at variable rates which move inversely with the prices received in international markets, or the establishment of export marketing boards can have an evening effect on the prices or earnings of producers. Such policies will relieve the individual producer from the risks and burdens of instability, but usually at the cost of destabilizing the government revenue. The destabilizing effect on the internal economy therefore seems difficult to avoid by such fiscal measures. Temporarily high profits in the export sector can of course be taxed away, so as to avoid excessive demand pressures. But while it is comparatively easy to increase the taxes or other levies on primary commodity producers and to adjust public expenditures to the high level of government revenue during periods of rising export proceeds, the government will be in a difficult situation when export revenues are shrinking. The depressed export sector would then need a tax reduction or a subsidy. As the government has no ready alternative source of revenue, while it may have committed itself to planned expenditure over several years, it cannot relieve the burden from the export sector, unless it is willing to accept an underbalanced budget, with ensuing inflationary pressures as the likely result. The experiences of many Latin American countries point to this problem.

The u-country government which pursues internal stabilization measures during a period of unstable export revenue, while simultaneously carrying on an ambitious development plan, will also have to tackle the problem of unstable exchange availability. The instabilities in both government revenue and in exchange earnings will make it difficult to pursue long-term development plans, and it seems reasonable to argue that they will decrease the efficiency of development policy.

To ensure a steady availability of exchange for the implementation of long-term planning, a great number of u-countries have given preference to imports of capital goods by the introduction of exchange and import controls. To step up the development pace, some countries have gone so far as to discontinue almost all "non-essential" imports. The planning problems in those countries become still more difficult if, after they have succeeded with this objective, they are faced with a further fall in export revenue. There are then no "non-essential" imports to be cut, and the maintenance of the plan will become dependent on loans or grants from abroad; and if these are not forthcoming, devaluation will sometimes be the only way of securing the foreign exchange which is required.

Problems in reaching optimal resource allocation decisions, higher average unemployment, insecurity for small commodity-producers, difficulties in the implementation of long-term economic plans, exchange and import controls, instability in internal prices and in government revenue and devaluation - these appear to be the main negative effects of excessive export instability in u-countries. These are then the reasons why u-countries urge international action to stabilize the commodity markets. If such stabilization becomes an international responsibility, then the u-country governments should be relieved of the problems enumerated here. If, in addition, the commodity arrangements are so constructed that the aid flow is increased, so as to counter the allegedly falling commodity terms of trade, then the development process can be further speeded up by the additional resources which are made available.

The views presented here on the negative effects of export instability to u-countries have recently been challenged in a few empirical studies, which fail to find any significant correlation between export instability and any important domestic variables. The results of these studies, and some of their implications for international commodity arrangements, will be taken up in the last chapter.

II.3   <u>The threat of synthetics</u>

The principal natural products currently facing serious competition from synthetic materials are rubber, cotton and wool, jute, hard fibres, tropical oils and oil seeds used in detergents, and hides and skins. In addition, sugar and some spices are being threatened by synthetic products, while plastic goods replace a number of commodities, like timber, metals, leather and hard fibres in various uses. Research is also going on to bring out further synthetic goods to replace commodities, the most noteworthy being perhaps coffee. The emergence of synthetics usually starts on a small scale and at relatively high prices. After the initial period, prices tend to decrease very considerably, and stabilize, while output continues to grow at a high rate. The following figures indicate the fast growth of production and the total market share of two by now well-established synthetic materials: [10]

	Total consumption (million metric tons)	As % of total fibre and rubber consumption by value
Man-made fibres:		
1953-55	1.6	32
1959-61	2.3	44
1964-66	3.8	61
Synthetic fibres:		
1953-55	0.9	38
1959-61	1.7	54
1964-66	2.7	63

The inroad of synthetics into the natural commodity markets obviously creates a number of adverse consequences for the latter. The effects on total production will depend on the growth of demand as a whole. If this is increasing at a high rate, there may be room left for expansion of the natural commodity in spite of the fast growth of synthetic production. The above figures, for instance, indicate a small absolute increase for natural rubber consumption in the period considered. The introduction of synthetics may in some cases not merely result in a division of the existing market, but in view of the specific features of the synthetic, an expansion of uses outside that of the natural commodity may also take place, and thus widen the total available market. The stability of synthetic prices after the initial introduction period (US synthetic rubber prices, for instance, remained unchanged between 1953 and 1962)[11] is a priori likely to increase the stability of commodities which compete with synthetics. This is because the susceptibility to substitution will increase the price elasticity of demand for the natural commodity, and small price variations will be sufficient to bring about large changes in the quantity demanded. Such a tendency has been observable in the case of rubber, but hard fibre prices have continued to vary sharply in spite of competition from nylon and other man-made fibres.

Where synthetics are already established, the competitive situation is usually dependent on the differences in price or in quality, and sometimes in both. Where price competition is predominant, as in the case of rubber, the problem of the commodity producers is to maintain or lower prices. For this an increase in productivity is usually required. Research and development has tremendously expanded the potential productivity of rubber trees, but in practice improvements are slow because of the relatively long life of the tree. Technical improvements in synthetic production have so far maintained a cost advantage for synthetic rubber. Furthermore, the research into synthetics gradually improves their quality. In view of this, the natural product prices would have to decline if producers are to maintain their market shares.

Alternatively, the synthetic product is in some way superior to the natural commodity, and competitive strength depends more on this qualitative difference than on price. Nylon versus hard fibres may be used as an illustration. The appropriate policy for the natural commodity producers in this case would be to improve the characteristics of their product by better extraction, new varieties or improved processing. Further measures may be to standardize grading or look into and suggest alternative uses, in which the natural commodity is superior to the synthetic one.

A competitive advantage possessed by most synthetic materials is price stability, predictable and ensured supply, and definite quality standards. The fact that synthetic production is usually situated in the countries of further processing and final use, makes it relatively simple to integrate the various stages of the production process. This is common in rubber, where production of the raw material and tyre manufacturing is often in the same ownership, or in textiles, where fibres and weave are sometimes produced by the same establishment. This creates the so-called "captive markets", to which entry for foreign natural commodity producers is closed.

A further difficulty arises from the fact that for economic or strategic reasons i-countries tend to protect their synthetic production, often at rates which increase with the stage of processing of the commodity, which makes the effective tariff on processing more or less prohibitive.

On account of the arguments enumerated here, one would expect, on the whole, decreasing price trends for commodities facing competition from substitutes, in comparison with commodities in general. The figures presented below show for the period 1953-66 the averages of the year-to-year percentage changes in the prices of some commodities with synthetic substitutes: [12]

		%
1.	Jute	+4.5
2.	Sisal	+3.2
3.	Copra and coconut oil	-0.2
4.	Sugar	-0.2
5.	Rubber	-1.1
6.	Hides and skins	-1.2
7.	Wool	-1.4
8.	Cotton	-2.9

Table II.2   Importance of exports from selected u-countries of major agricultural materials subject to competition from synthetics, 1964.

Country	Total exports (million $)	Proportion of total exports in % for						
		cotton	wool	jute	hard fibres	natural rubber	hides and skins	total 6 comm. groups
Chad	27	78					2	80
Pakistan	493	25	3	49			1	78
Rep. of Vietnam	48					69		69
UAR	539	60						60
Syria	176	50	5				1	56
Sudan	198	47					1	48
Tanzania	197	14			31		2	47
Uruguay	179		38				9	47
Nicaragua	118	44						44
Malaysia	1.125					41		41

Source: UNCTAD: Commodity Trade and Policies TD/27, 20 Nov., 1967, stencil, p.6-7.

Over the same period the average yearly change in all primary
commodity prices was approximately -0.4%.[13]   Although larger
price decreases predominate for the above commodities, no definite conclusions can be drawn from this material.

The severity of synthetic substitution for individual countries will
depend on the extent to which their exports contain commodities
competing with synthetics. This dependence is illustrated by the
figures in Table II.2 which is an excerpt from material collected
by UNCTAD. Only countries whose share of such exports exceeds
40% are reproduced here.

We should remember that what the figures convey is the actual
position. The potential threat from future synthetic materials
could be much more important for producing countries.

The research into and emergence of synthetics is usually initiated
by high prices or uncertain supply of the natural materials. Dis-
satisfaction with some qualitative features of the natural commodity
may also be the cause for search of alternative solutions. The
conclusion to be drawn from this is that the likelihood for further
emergence of synthetics could be diminished by vigorous productivity drives coupled with cautious pricing policies, by measures to
ensure stability of supply and by more intensive product development aiming at better satisfaction of the users' needs.

Off and on, international conferences express resolutions suggesting that i-countries' research efforts to bring out synthetic
substitutes for natural commodities should be slowed down. This
is an understandable recommendation from countries heavily
dependent on commodity exports and with limited ability to diversify their economy. From the consumers' point of view, such
recommendations seem highly dubious. Synthetics which can
economize on the resources used in production are naturally
desirable. If their appearance leads to external diseconomies,
depressing the conditions of primary producers, then temporary
subsidies and transfers seem to be the appropriate measure.
But here we leave the problem of efficiency and enter that of equity.

II.4   The three approaches to commodity market arrangements

Broadly speaking, the international solutions to the commodity
market problems have been sought along three lines, which in a
somewhat stereotyped way could be called the Anglo-Saxon, the

Socialist Block and the French approaches. We will deal now predominantly with what is here called the <u>Anglo-Saxon</u> approach. This has by and large been the approach adopted by the UN, and has had as its aim broad, international commodity arrangements with as little direct intervention as possible in the functioning of commodity markets. Despite the tendency in the USA and the UK towards generalized trade relations, these two countries are maintaining sizeable preferential arrangements for several commodities, for instance sugar.[14] The preferential tariffs within the Commonwealth also constitute a deviation from the generally proclaimed aims. Before proceeding further in the study of this approach, at least a few words should be mentioned about the other two.

The <u>Socialist Block</u> policy in commodity markets has been characterized by long-term bilateral agreements with a number of u-countries, providing for steady and increasing trade volume,[15] and on the other hand, violently fluctuating commodity sales to the Western i-countries. The latter policy has been caused partly by commercial warfare tactics, and partly by fluctuating exchange needs, particularly in the Soviet Union. These aspects will not be further discussed here.

The long-term bilateral agreements between the Socialist Block and u-countries have, until the beginning of the 1960's, stipulated a complete balance of trade between each pair of countries. Since then, the agreements have become more flexible in permitting certain short-term credit facilities to each side.[16] The agreements contain clauses on goods to be included in the exports. The accounting prices are reviewed at regular intervals, usually taking the world price developments as a basis when revision is undertaken. Often the agreements contain an element of aid, although this is somewhat difficult to establish and calculate.

To u-countries there are many advantages from long-term contracts of this type. In particular, the bilateral agreements make it easier for u-countries to plan ahead with their development programs. Consequently their trade with the Socialist countries has increased very fast. Between 1954 and 1965, the value of their exports to the Socialist Block increased by an average of 15% per year, to be compared with a mere 4% for exports to developed market economies excluding Japan. The absolute figures for this Socialist Block trade, however, are still comparatively small. By 1965, u-countries' exports to Socialist countries amounted to some $2 billion, compared with about $26 billion for developed market economies excluding Japan. [17]   If this trend continues, u-countries' trade with the Socialist Block will with time become much more important.

Two disadvantages are connected with the Socialist approach to commodity trade with u-countries. The first is that a particular Socialist country has only a limited range of goods to offer in return for u-countries' commodities. The capital equipment needed for a u-country's development program may not be available in the Socialist country with which the agreement has been signed. Without the agreement, the u-country could have sold its commodity in the international market, possibly at lower prices, but with payment in convertible currency, which could be used for purchases anywhere. The bilateral agreement deprives it of this liberty.   The second disadvantage is caused by the Socialist resales in the Western markets of commodities imported from u-countries. Indian textiles and Cuban sugar have thus been sold at low prices in Western Europe, in competition with these two countries' direct export to the West European market.

France maintains rather intricate trade relations with the Franc Zone countries. [18]   Prices far above the world market levels are in many cases paid in imports and exports of various commodities. Arrangements for imports into Metropolitan France and re-exports into another Franc Zone country are also in force.

Since 1961, in various international gatherings, France has made proposals about international commodity arrangements. [19]   These proposals have never been put forward in the form of a detailed and comprehensive plan, but three important themes have been: [20]

1. Market organization for temperate zone agricultural products aiming at higher prices on the world market.

2. Use of surpluses of temperate zone products in a program for accelerated development of u-countries.

3. Market organization for non-agricultural and tropical agricultural commodities, aiming at higher prices.

The main argument is to raise all commodity prices in order to increase the earnings of u-countries. One way of doing this would be to let u-countries export commodities to i-countries at the domestic prices in the latter. Alternatively, i-countries might tax their commodity imports and hand over the tax proceeds to u-countries. In what follows, the case of wheat will be taken to illustrate the rather complicated French stand.

The underlying idea is that the low prices of the residual world wheat market do not cover the production costs of a majority of wheat producers, and therefore most production for world trade has to be subsidized. Consequently, wheat exporter governments are subsidizing the wheat importing countries. To rectify this situation, wheat prices in the international market should be considerably increased, at least so that all major producers' costs are covered. This is a somewhat surprising statement in view of the depressing long-term price prospects for wheat. Furthermore, the increased income of the wheat exporting countries from their exports to i-countries should be used for shipment of wheat free of charge or on very advantageous terms to u-countries, and thus contribute to a considerable increase in international development aid. To prevent an excessive increase in wheat production in the exporting countries, the governments of these might suitably tax wheat export sales to i-countries, so that the additional sales proceeds do not reach individual producers.

A number of intricate problems appear on a proper scrutiny of the French wheat proposals. To operate them, one would probably have to establish a system of commercial operations with export quotas for i-markets and an undertaking for the importers to buy. In addition, the exporting countries would have to agree to use their higher proceeds from the wheat sales to finance concessional wheat shipments to u-countries. In the final analysis, the scheme amounts to a very complicated transfer of resources from i- to u-countries, where it would be difficult to determine who pays how much for the resource transfer. The effects on the commodity markets are difficult to predict, but could be considerable and burdensome. [21)]   The same aid transfer could be achieved by much simpler means.

Notes and references to Chapter II

1) UNCTAD I, New York 1964, Proceedings, Vol. III, p. 143.

2) M. Michaely, Concentration in International Trade, Amsterdam 1962, Ch. 2.

3) UNCTAD I, New York 1964, Proceedings, Vol. III, p. 111.

4) For a discussion of the taxation problems in u-countries, see for instance W. W. Heller, Fiscal policies for underdeveloped economies, Harvard Law School, Cambridge, 1954.

5) For a survey of the activities of existing marketing boards, see FAO: Agricultural Marketing Boards, Rome, 1966.

6) H. C. Wallich, 'Stabilization of proceeds from raw material exports'; from Howard Ellis, Economic development for Latin America, New York, 1961.

7) S. Caine, 'Instability of primary product prices', Economic Journal, Sept. 1954.

8) See for instance R. Nurkse, 'Trade fluctuations and buffer policies of low income countries', Kyklos, 1958, p. 141-154.

9) For a more detailed analysis of the inflexibilities of underdeveloped economies, and their effects on trade and transformation, see H. Myint, 'The Classical Theory of International Trade, and The Underdeveloped Countries', Economic Journal, June 1958.

10) UNCTAD: Commodity Problems and Policies, TD/27, 20 Nov., 1967, stencil, p. 3.

11) UNCTAD I, New York 1964, Proceedings, Vol. III, p. 354.

12) UNCTAD: Commodity Problems and Policies, TD/9, stencil, 10 Nov., 1967, chart 2.

13) UN Yearbook for International Trade Statistics and UN Statistical Yearbook.

14) See section III. 2 on the sugar agreement.

15) For an exposition of the Soviet Block trade relations with u-countries, see UNCTAD: Trends and Problems in World Trade and Development, TD/18/suppl 2, stencil, 29 Dec., 1967.

16) In addition, the Socialist countries have exported various goods to u-countries on both long and short credit terms, sometimes with repayment in convertible currencies, in other cases against future commodity exports from u-countries.

17) Figures from UNCTAD: Review of International Trade and Development, 1967, TD/5, stencil, 15 Nov., 1967, p.28-29.

18) The Franc Zone includes, aside from France, mainly former French colonies in Africa.

19) For a summary see UNCTAD I, New York 1964, Proceedings, Vol.III, p.486-494.

20) UNCTAD I, New York 1964, Proceedings, Vol.III, article by Hooft-Welvaars, p.459.

21) For a study of the consequences of an incoherent market regulation, see for instance Bentzel, Lindbeck, Stahl, Bostadsbristen, IUI, Stockholm 1963, which describes the conditions on the Swedish housing market.

III. THE EXPERIENCE OF COMMODITY AGREEMENTS AFTER 1945

III.1 <u>Brief historical review</u>

The first commodity agreements date back to the beginning of this century. Up to the world crisis of 1930, the agreements were usually concluded between producers' groups only. In the 1930's, governments became more active in supporting the primary industries of their countries. This gave the agreements greater weight and discipline. The brief review of commodity agreements up to World War II which now follows is intended as a background to the discussion of post-war international schemes.

Since the beginning of this century, Brazil has provided the world market with a very substantial share of all internationally traded <u>coffee</u>. In view of sharp crop fluctuations, unilateral attempts were made by Brazil on several occasions to establish buffer stocks, to bridge over the year-to-year swings. The first scheme of this type dates back to 1907, and was followed by several others. The variations of supply were coupled with large over-production during certain periods, and the buffer scheme suffered substantial losses in the Great Depression. New attempts in the 1930's, with other producing countries participating, ended in world over-production, a drastic price fall, and the famous destruction of Brazilian coffee stocks by using them as fuel.

Canada's importance in the world market as an exporter of <u>wheat</u> in the 1920's was similar to that of Brazil in coffee. In 1928 the Canadian wheat pools were organized, to centralize marketing and to establish buffers in good crop years. During the Great Depression the Canadian and US governments interfered in their countries' wheat markets to arrest the continuous downward price trend, which threatened to result in social unrest. In 1933 an international wheat agreement was reached, with export quotas as the main operative tool. This was the first agreement in which importing countries took an active part.

In 1926, the Government of Cuba undertook to organize the small sugar producers of the country with a view to restricting exports and arresting the falling prices. In 1931 Cuba along with Java reached an export quota agreement with several European exporters. It proved impossible to limit the supply, because producers outside the agreement substantially increased their production.

The main tea-producing countries operated an export quota scheme in the 1930's. An unusual feature was that the export quotas were freely marketable.

The period immediately following World War I saw a heavy fall in rubber prices. The producers of Malaya and Ceylon agreed on an export restriction scheme, which succeeded in substantially raising prices. After some time, the scheme ran into difficulties due to consumer resistance, particularly from US manufacturing industries, and because of increased outside production, notably by Java. It was dissolved during the Depression. A new export restriction scheme was introduced around 1933.

After World War I the copper- and tin-mining industries operated buffer stock schemes to damp down price fluctuations. From 1926 onwards the International Copper Cartel came into operation and its policies resulted in substantial price increases. The cartel was relatively easy to operate, as there were few owners of copper-mining industries, and 75% of the capital in copper mines was owned by US interests. The cartel broke during the Wall Street crash in 1929. In the 1930's new agreements came into force both for copper in the form of export quota control, and for tin by maintenance of a buffer stock.

In the period after 1945, in line with the procedures and principles agreed upon by the UN Havana Conference in 1947-8, commodity agreements usually have an equal representation of producing and consuming interests. As a result, the earlier post-war agreements have put less emphasis on maintenance of over-high prices, as compared with conditions in the 1930's. In view of consumers' participation, the post-war agreements have had a much better chance to influence the demand side of the market. The participation of consuming interests has, on the other hand, made it much more difficult to negotiate and reach agreements. During the entire post-war period only a few commodities have been regulated by international schemes. These will be reviewed below.

40

III.2 <u>Sugar</u>

Sugar is a commodity produced both in temperate and tropical countries. The cost of production of cane sugar is usually lower than
that of beet sugar. Thus u-countries have a comparative advantage
in sugar production.[1]   Temperate zone i-countries maintain a
sizeable beet-sugar production with the help of tariffs and other
import restrictions. In 1961-2 the degree of self-sufficiency was
estimated at 88% in Europe, including the USSR, and 33% in the
USA. The percentages are higher than the pre-war levels, and have
been gradually increasing in the post-war period.[2]

Table III.1   <u>World production and exports of centrifugal sugar</u>

   (million tons)

	Average 1953-55	1957-61	1962	1963	1964	1965	1966	1967	1968[*]
Production	39	48	51	55	66	66	63	65	66
Exports	14	17	19	18	18	20	19	21	-

[*] Estimated

Source: FAO Commodity Review 1966 and 1968.

Exports of sugar constitute about 30% of total world production. For
a long time a considerable share of world exports has been directed
under preferential treatment to the USA, the Commonwealth and to
a lesser extent to the Franc Zone.[3]   (Preferential prices in 1965
for exports to the USA were 6.75 cts/pound, and to the UK 5.80 cts/
pound, according to FAO Commodity Review, 1966). In 1959-61
more than a third of total exports were sold under preferential
arrangements at relatively stable prices much above the remaining
"free" world market. In the preferential market, the USA accounted
for 3.5 million tons in 1959-61 and for 3.4 in 1966, while Commonwealth figures were 2.2 and 1.7 million tons respectively for the
same years. Sugar exports from Cuba to the Eastern Block, also
governed by long-term agreements, account for another 3 million
tons.[4]

Table III.2   Some important sugar exporting countries

(Exports, million tons)

	1960	1967
Australia	0.8	1.7
Cuba	5.6	6.1
Dominican Republic	1.1	0.7
France	0.6	0.5
Mauritius	0.3	0.5
Mexico	0.4	0.6
Poland	0.3	0.9
South Africa	0.9	0.6

Source: FAO Monthly Bulletin, May 1966 and November 1968.
          FAO Commodity Review 1968.

The free market, with which international agreements have been
concerned, accounts for about 15% of world production and less than
half of world exports. The total value of this trade was estimated
in 1959-61 at $500 million.[4]

Attempts at regulating international sugar trade date as far back as
1902. In the post-war period five year agreements were signed in
1954 and 1959 with gradually increasing numbers of exporting and
importing countries as members. From 1959 onwards, all the
major exporting and importing countries were participating.[5] The
second agreement was merely a continuation of the first. The
International Sugar Council was established, to convene conferences
and operate the agreements. Export quotas and exporter stocks
between prescribed limits have been used as the methods of control
of the sugar market.

The basic quotas were distributed among participating exporters
mainly on a historical basis. Proportional changes in the quotas
were to regulate the quantities to be traded. From 1957 the quotas
were left unchanged as long as the price remained within the range
of 3.25 and 3.75 US cents per pound. At prices above 3.75, the
Council was allowed gradually to increase the quotas, until the
price level reached 4.00, when all export control was withdrawn,
and importing members were simultaneously released from their
obligation to buy exclusively from exporting members. When the
price fell below 3.25, the Council was empowered to cut basic
quotas, but in no case by more than 20%.[6]

D

In addition to the influence exerted by the export quotas, production
was to be regulated by provisions about carry-over stocks. The
stocks would also cushion the year-to-year crop fluctuations. The
agreement stipulated exporter stocks of at least 10% of basic export
quotas, but not exceeding 12.5% of the previous year's output, at
the time just before the harvest. [6)]

The measures of control seem to have been inadequate to provide
for price stability within the desired range, and still less to influence the long-term price trend. Throughout the period of the
agreements, stocks in the major exporting countries frequently
exceeded the stipulated maxima, which seems to be an indication of
the exporting countries' inability to limit production, and of a
consequent over-supply.

In 1960, the international sugar market was severely disrupted by
the fact that the USA completely cut Cuba's preferential quota,
amounting to nearly 1.4 million tons, and instead imported equivalent amounts from other countries, under preferential tariffs
outside the international agreement. The 1960-1 world crop was
unusually large, and prices occasionally dropped to about 2.00 cents
per pound. When the International Sugar Conference met towards
the end of 1961 to readjust the basic quotas within the 1959-64
agreement, no accord could be reached, particularly in view of the
Cuban demands, and the agreement ceased to function.

Chart III.1 shows the development of prices in the international
sugar market.

Conclusions about the effects of the agreement are very difficult to
draw. It may be interesting to note that, both during and after the
cessation of the agreement, the peak prices are correlated with
political disturbances, temporarily pushing up demand, rather than
reflecting disequilibria of consumption over supply. Thus the peak
in 1951 reflects the Korean war boom, the high levels in 1956 and
1957, the Suez crisis, while the 1963 sky-rocket seems to be a result
of the Cuba crisis.

Following the negotiations at UNCTAD II in New Delhi in 1968, a
new sugar agreement was reached in October of that year. The new
agreement is primarily based on export restrictions, and supported
by importing members' obligations not to import from non-member

<u>Chart III.1</u>   <u>Sugar, movements of prices</u>

1948-51 f.a.s. Cuba
1952-60 f.o.b. Cuba
1961-   ISC price, f.a.s. Cuban port basis

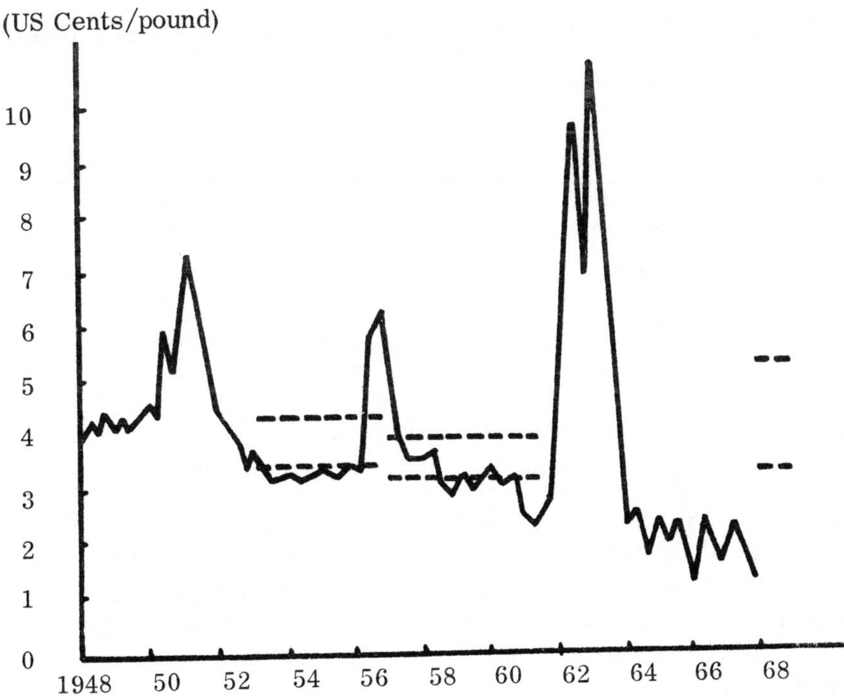

(The dotted lines indicate the Sugar Council's price ranges.)

<u>Sources</u>: 1948-63 from UNCTAD I, New York 1964. Proceedings,
Vol. III.
1964-68 from FAO Monthly Bulletin.

exporters, and to keep a definite part of their domestic markets
open to imports. The price range to be defended by this agreement
is between 3.3 and 5.2 cents per pound. A considerable weakness
of this agreement is that neither the USA nor the EEC are participating.[7]

III.3 Tin

Internationally traded tin and tin concentrates account for over 80% of world production, and were valued in 1962 at about 350 million US $. The u-countries' share of this trade constitutes around 75%. [8]   Statistics for the main producing countries appear from Table III.3.

Table III.3   Main producers of tin concentrates in metal equivalent (thousand tons)

	1960	1967
World	139	172
Bolivia	21	27
China mainland	24	-
Indonesia	23	14
Malaysia	53	72
Thailand	12	23

Source: UN Statistical Yearbook 1965, p.200.
International Tin Council Statistical Bulletin.

Although most tin mining takes place in u-countries, it should be noted that many of the mines are owned by West European and North American interests. Several West European countries, notably Belgium, Holland and the UK are large-scale importers of concentrates, while they export tin. [8]   The Second World War had a considerable effect on tin consumption. The scarcity which resulted from the Japanese occupation of Malaysia and Indonesia brought with it an increased use of substitutes, and new techniques which saved on the consumption of tin. [9]   These developments have naturally also influenced post-war conditions.

Soon after the war, discussions on an international tin agreement were taken up in accordance with the UN-Havana Charter, with exporter and consumer interests amply represented. Before any agreement had been reached, the Korean war broke out, with all its upsetting effects on commodity prices. Not until 1956 was it possible to reach a general agreement between the main exporting and importing countries, and even then neither the USA, a large importer, nor the USSR, an important exporter, joined. The agreement extended over 5 years, and was renegotiated in 1960 and 1966 for similar periods.

Similar to the case of sugar, the tin agreement is intended to maintain price stability through varying export quotas and maintenance of buffer stocks. In the tin agreement it is the centrally-operated buffer stock, which is to play the primary stabilizing role. The International Tin Council, representing in 1966 6 exporting and 16 importing countries, which account for a very large proportion of total tin production and trade, decides on the policy of the scheme. A price range is defined and the stock controller, appointed by the council, is given the task to purchase and sell so as to maintain prices within the range. If prices are in the middle sector of the range, the controller has to be passive; if in the upper or lower sectors, he is allowed to buy or sell; while he is forced to buy or sell if prices move outside the range. The initial price range was between £640 and £880 per ton. Later developments of the range can be seen from Chart III.2. The financial resources needed by the controller were supplied by the exporting countries, and initially amounted to £16 million, equivalent to 25,000 tons at the floor price, to be provided either in metal or in cash. [10)]   Later, the controller's resources were increased to £20 million and made more elastic by a credit facility of £10 million. [11)] If the stock of tin exceeds a certain amount, the council is empowered to impose export quota restrictions, proportional to historical export quantities from the various countries.

Nothing is said in the agreement about importing members' obligations to buy exclusively from exporting members; importing members' only responsibility seems to be to make contributions to cover the administrative expenditures of the council and to help finance the buffer stock, the latter on a voluntary basis.

The resources at the disposal of the tin stock controller have been far too limited to exert proper influence in the market. As can be seen from Table III.4 below, the buffer stocks constitute only a small proportion of total stocks in the few years when any stocks at all are available within the scheme.

The international tin market should be easier to control than, for example, sugar, in view of the high proportion of the total world trade taking place within the framework of the agreement, and the fact that the number of producers is much more restricted; however, there is another condition, which has made tin control very difficult, namely the instability of US strategic stockpiling. In the

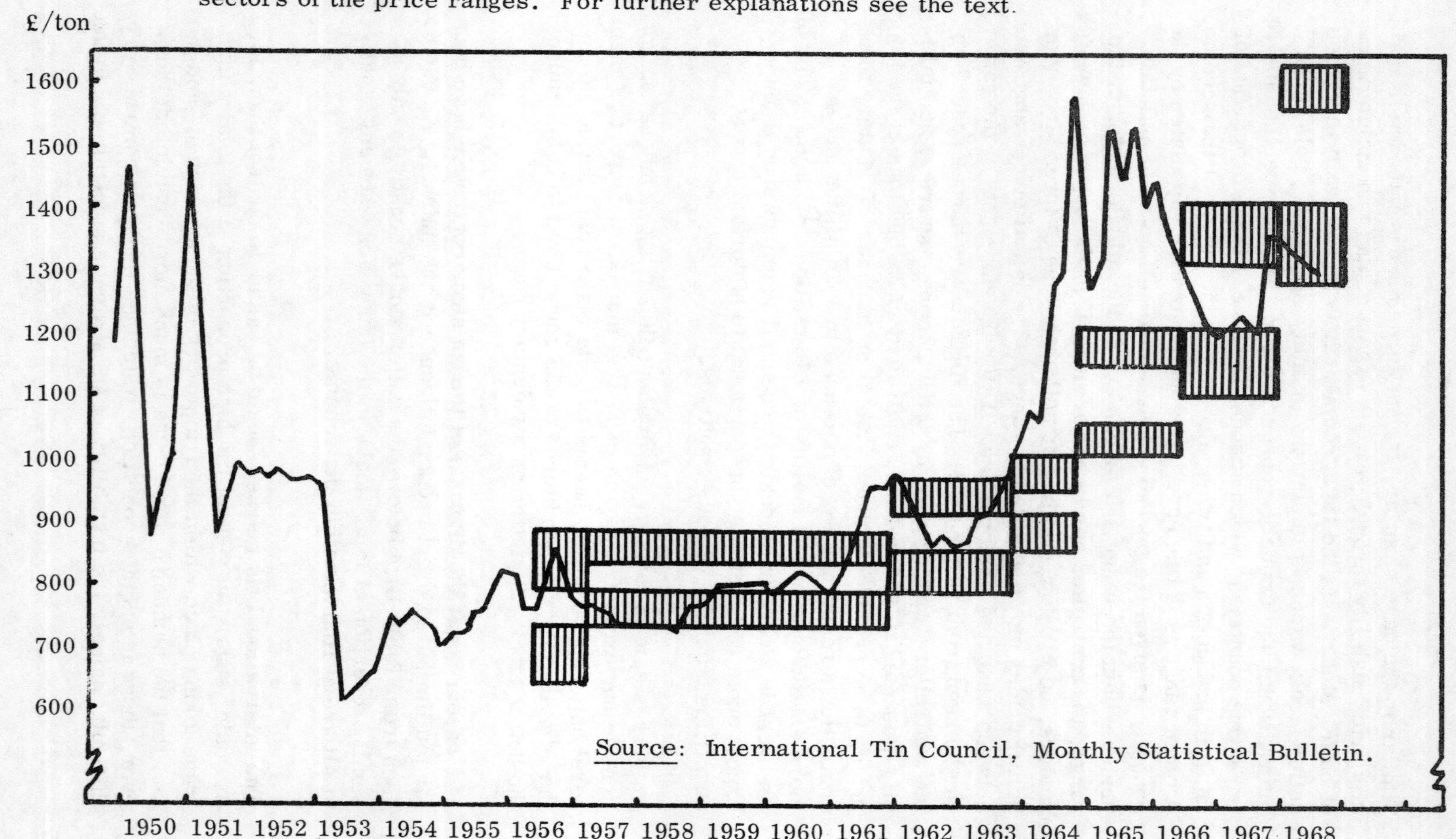

Chart III.2   Tin prices. LME, cash, £/ton, monthly average and price ranges in the tin agreements. Shaded areas indicate the upper and lower sectors of the price ranges. For further explanations see the text.

Source: International Tin Council, Monthly Statistical Bulletin.

Table III.4   **Stocks of tin metal**

(thousand tons)

World, excluding ITA buffer and US strategic stockpile	Dec.	1956	1957	1958	1959	1960	1961
		44.6	59.4	59.7	63.5	63.5	56.5
		1962	1963	1964	1965	1966	1967	Mar. 1968
		51.3	46.8	50.4	52.1	51.4	53.3	–

ITA buffer	Dec.	1956	1957	1958	1959	1960	1961
		0	15.3	23.3	10.1	10.0	0
		1962	1963	1964	1965	1966	1967	Mar. 1968
		3.2	0	0	0	0	4.8	8.2

Source: International Tin Council Statistical Yearbook 1964 and ITC Monthly Statistical Bulletin.

beginning of 1962, US strategic stocks were announced to be about 350,000 tons, equivalent to more than 2 years' world production, and of this more than 150,000 tons were declared to be surplus to requirements. [12]

Although consultations have been taking place off and on between the Tin Council and representatives of the US strategic stock, it has not been possible to persuade the US government to co-operate fully within the terms of the international agreement. [13]

Table III.5   **Releases from US Strategic stockpiles**

(tons)

1962	1963	1964	1965	1966	1967
1.001	9,934	28,615	23,987	16,175	4,923

Source: International Tin Council Statistical Bulletin.

Some authors seem to conclude that US stockpile sales contributed to the instability of the tin market, and that after 1962 the USA had taken over the role of the International agreement as the main price influencing factor in the market.[12] As can be seen from Chart III.2 the price of tin showed a slow but definite upward trend for a number of years before US releases were started. Contrary to what one would expect, the year 1964, when US releases reached a maximum, coincides with sharp price increases. Quite certainly tin prices would have increased still further if the US sales had not taken place at that time.

Since the establishment of the tin agreement, it is, with the exception of 1964 and 1965, only on a few occasions, and for limited periods, that prices have moved outside the agreed range. This is above all a result of the scheme's considerable flexibility with regard to price changes and the width of the price range.[14]

III.4 <u>Wheat</u>

Total world wheat production has been gradually increasing from around 200 million tons in 1953-56 to about 300 in the later sixties. During the same period exports have almost doubled and account for some 15% of total world production. In 1962 the value of international wheat trade amounted to more than $1 billion.

Table III.6   <u>World production and exports of wheat</u>

(million tons)

| | Averages | | | | | | | | |
	1953-56	1957-62	1962	1963	1964	1965	1966	1967	1968
Production	202	241	264	245	273	256	308	297	315[*]
Exports	26	35	40	55	50	48	51	40	-

[*] estimated

Source: FAO Commodity Review 1966 and 1968.
FAO Monthly Bulletin.

Surpluses of production over consumption are confined to a few i-countries, notably the USA, Canada and Australia. During recent years, the USA and Canada have accounted for more than 60% of total world exports. [15)]

All major industrial countries have built up a heavy protection for their internal wheat production. The protective measures stimulate production in the countries which use them. Imports become of marginal importance, and in some cases, e.g. France or Sweden, the policy leads to a reversal into large subsidized exports. [16)] During most of the post-war period, world production has been exceeding consumption, resulting in a build-up of sizeable stocks. [16)] In the mid-1960's, the world wheat balance was temporarily restored by two new developments. One was the large net imports of China and the USSR, the latter having earlier been a net exporter, and the very high volume of international wheat shipments to u-countries on concessional terms.

A series of international wheat agreements have been in operation since 1949. Parties to the agreements have been the major export-ing and importing countries, with important exceptions during certain periods, e.g. the UK, Argentina or the USSR. The coverage of trade under the agreements has not been very complete, and the relative stability of wheat prices must be explained by other factors. [17)]

The technique of operation of the wheat agreements has undergone an important change in 1959. Until then the controlling instrument consisted of an undertaking by the exporters to sell guaranteed quantities not above a fixed maximum price, and a reciprocal obli-gation for the importers to buy specified amounts at prices above given minimums. The agreements had no provisions for stock-keeping, and members were free to trade as they wished outside their quota obligations. From 1959 onwards, the system of speci-fied quotas was discontinued. Instead, the importing members undertook to buy a fixed proportion of their commercial imports from exporting members at prices at or above a specified minimum. The obligation of the exporters was now to sell to the importing member at or below the maximum of the price range an amount equal to the average of their last four years' exports to member countries. [17)] Thus there is no longer any direct reciprocity between importers' and exporters' obligations. During the period July 1967-June 1968, no agreement was in force. The agreement which has operated since July 1968 has established new price ranges, but operates in the main as the earlier ones. Chart III.3 indicates the wheat price variations, and also gives the price ranges of the wheat agreements.

Chart III.3   Wheat: Movement of prices and IWC price range

No.1. Manitoba, Northern (Class II) in bulk, in store Fort William, Canada. Monthly averages.

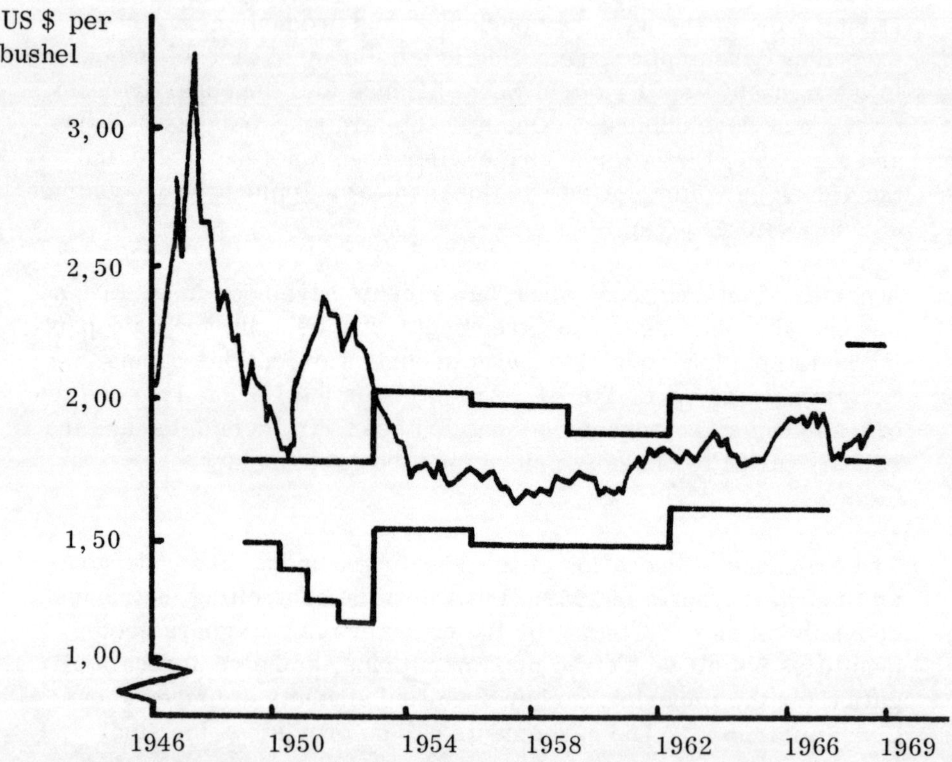

Sources: UNCTAD I, New York 1964, Proceedings, Vol.III, p.134.
IWC World wheat statistics, 1966.
FAO Monthly Statistical Bulletin.
FAO Commodity Review 1968.

As appears from the chart, market prices outside the agreed quotas remained above the agreed price range throughout the period of the first agreement, which ended in 1953. The exporters fulfilled their obligations, and prices of wheat traded within the agreement remained at the maximum of the range. According to Rowe[18] the price developments in the "free" market did not properly reflect conditions of demand and supply. In fact, wheat stocks in the USA and Canada more than doubled from 1952 to 1953.[19] If the increase in production had been able to affect the market, price developments would have been quite different. In reality, the US internal price support policy for wheat established the US free export price at about $2.20 per bushel, with the result that Canada and other major exporting countries followed the US price leadership, and fixed their own export prices immediately below that of the USA. Good harvests in both exporting and importing countries in 1953-4, and a consequent reduction of importer demand, induced the USA to decrease its export prices to $1.70-1.80 per bushel, well within the newly agreed price range. The world market followed, and the prices have remained at about the same level ever since.

The role of the agreements in maintaining price stability has gradually diminished, and has been replaced by price administration from the two main exporting countries, the USA and Canada.[20] The price maintenance above market equilibrium has compelled the USA to take measures to contract production by limiting wheat acreage, and both the North American exporters have been forced to keep heavy stocks.

Table III.7   Wheat stocks

(million tons)

	1950	1955	1960	1965	1968/69
USA and Canada	4.6	42.8	52.1	36.3	34
All major exporters	8.9	52.1	58.3	42.6	38

Source: UNCTAD I, New York 1964, Proceedings, Vol. III, p. 424 and 506.
FAO Commodity Review 1968.

For several years, wheat stocks in the USA and Canada exceeded one full year's world exports. Rather than allowing the price to fall further, the North American countries substantially increased their sales of wheat on concessional terms. In the mid-1960's these

concessional shipments from North America reached almost
20 million tons per year. The fall in the North American stocks in
later years, along with better harvests in South Asia, led to a
decrease of the concessional sales as well.

In the international wheat conference convened in 1967, some
thirteen rich wheat-exporting countries committed themselves to
contribute a total of 4.5 million tons per year as food aid gifts to
u-countries. The US share of this total is 42%, that of the EEC
23%. [21)

There is some reason to believe that the long-term prospects in
wheat are for heavily expanded production and falling prices. This
is mainly due to the technological breakthrough taking place in a
number of sub-tropical u-countries. New seed varieties, along with
higher inputs of fertilizer and a more reliable water supply through
irrigation, have drastically increased the per-acre output of pilot
areas in countries like Iran, Pakistan and India. Once the new seeds
and improved methods become widespread, several of the heavy
importers among u-countries may become self-sufficient, or even
net exporters, as a result of the ongoing "green revolution". [22)

III.5 <u>Coffee</u>

The sugar, tin, and wheat agreements, described above, differ
from the one affecting coffee in the sense that they all deal with
commodities, where i-countries have large interests in production,
in sugar and wheat through production in temperate zone i-countries,
in tin through ownership of mines and processing of concentrates
into metal. Coffee production and export, on the other hand, is the
exclusive interest of u-countries. The main coffee producers are
Brazil and Colombia in South America, and Angola, Ivory Coast
and Uganda in Africa. In 1964 Brazil's production amounted to 0.6
million tons, or about 20% of the world total. In 1959, the corresponding figures were 2.6 and 56%. [23) Frosts and crop diseases
are the main explanation of the violent changes. This volatile
supply pattern applies not only to Brazil, but to the world as a whole.
There is a close co-variation between damaged coffee harvests and
price peaks in the international coffee market.

As appears from Table III.8, a very high proportion of world production is exported. In 1962 the value of world exports was $1.7
billion.

Table III.8   Coffee. World production and exports

(million tons)

	Average 1957–61	1962	1963	1964	1965	1966	1967	1968[*]
Production	3.9	4.1	3.9	3.2	3.6	4.9	3.5	4.0
Exports	2.4	2.8	2.9	2.8	2.6	3.0	2.9	–

[*] preliminary

Source: FAO Commodity Review 1966 and 1968.

Violent harvest variations, coupled with considerable general over-production for long periods both before and after the Second World War, have resulted in sharp price fluctuations, on occasions at levels so low that some countries found it more advantageous to destroy the stocks which they had acquired, rather than to sell them and risk further price falls. After the Second World War, surplus problems started to be felt in the late 1950's, and attempts were made to limit exports by quota agreements between the main exporting countries.[24]   These efforts were concentrated to the period of price declines around 1957-8.

The international Exporter-Importer Coffee Agreement came into force in 1963, as a result of negotiations carried out under the auspices of the UN in 1962, with 36 exporting and 22 importing countries attending.[25]   In January 1964 the countries participating in the agreement accounted for over 99% of world exports and 95% of world imports of coffee.[26]   At an early stage in the negotiations, a consensus was reached that the new agreement would aim at maintaining coffee prices not lower than the 1962 level, that is about 35 cents per pound. According to Rowe[25] and Shishko[27], this was primarily a political move, initiated by the USA, to help the Latin American countries to increase and stabilize their exchange earnings.

The agreement operates primarily through quota adjustments for exports to member countries.[27]   Importers, on their part, are obliged to take all their import requirements from exporter members. In this way non-member producers are effectively cut out from all the important markets. Basic export quotas were originally

established at 2.7 million tons, in which the shares of Brazil and
Colombia were 1.08 and 0.36 tons respectively.[28] The adjustment
of coffee quotas to be undertaken annually has been left to the discretion of the International Coffee Council, in which exporting and
importing countries are represented by an equal number of votes.
A continuing and unresolved difficulty of the Coffee Council is the
competition among exporting members and their constant requests
for export quota revisions.[26] In recent years separate quotas
have been established for different varieties of coffee, mainly to
accommodate the increasing pressures of African producers. It has
also been proposed to introduce a maximum limit on the quantity
which member importers would accept to buy at the price level maintained by the agreement.[29] This underlines the impression that
the agreement price is above current market equilibrium.

Chart III.4   Coffee prices

Green Brazilian Santos 4, Spot New York

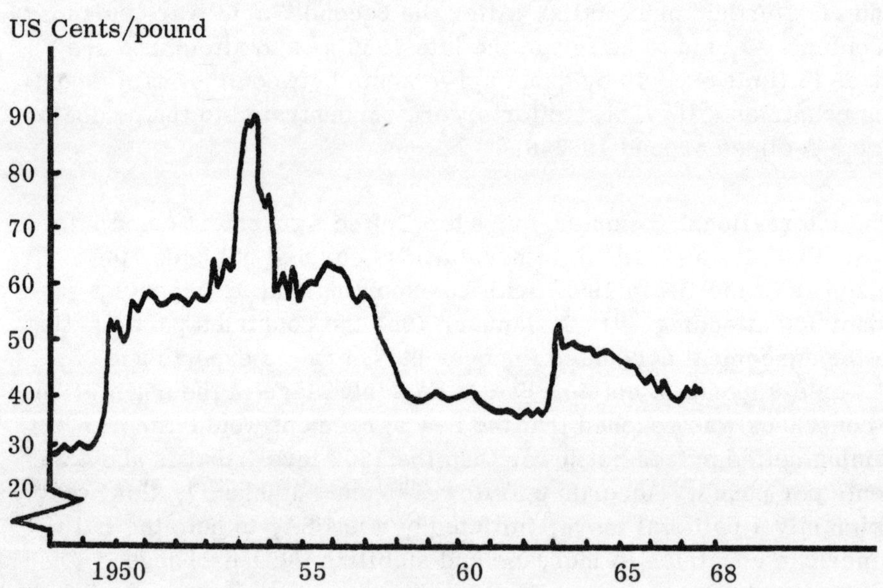

Sources: UNCTAD I, New York 1964, Proceedings, Vol. III, p. 133.
          FAO, Monthly Statistical Bulletin.

No price ranges have been fixed, and the Council's guideline in
adjusting quotas is the price level of 1962.

An additional feature of the Coffee Agreement is the "new" market, unregulated by the export quotas. The philosophy behind this division of the world into two markets is that in rich countries the price elasticity of demand is very low, and that therefore it is more profitable for exporting countries to control the supply through an agreement rather than through price competition. In the new markets, consisting primarily of u-countries (but also including the USSR), the price elasticity of demand is high, and consumption is likely to grow substantially if prices fall. Exporters are therefore allowed free competition in the new market.[30] A problem has been experienced with re-exports of coffee from the "new" to the established markets, and increasing efforts are made to enforce prohibition of such exports.

An extension for 5 years of the original agreement was signed in February 1968, without any important changes in the operative rules.

It is somewhat difficult to measure the degree of the coffee agreement's success, in terms of price levels achieved, because of the absence of established price ranges.

III.6 <u>International action in some other commodities</u>

<u>International producer agreements</u>

Since 1945 several agreements with exclusive exporter participation have functioned for limited periods. Two of the more important ones are briefly described below.

From 1943 till 1955 the major Asian <u>tea</u> exporters, along with their countries' governments, had an agreement aiming towards higher international prices through export quotas. Although production of tea has been increasing at a fast rate, the export quotas of the agreement were not fully utilized from about 1950 onwards. This is explained by a very steep rise in consumption in the producing countries, leaving smaller export surpluses.[31] When the agreement expired in 1955, it was not renewed.

Between 1964 and 1966, major producers' <u>copper</u> prices were deliberately kept below the London Metal Exchange quotations, in an attempt to slow down the substitution of other metals for copper. In

1966 the temptation became too strong for some of the producers to take advantage of the high LME prices. The agreement broke down, and as a result there was a sharp price fall in the LME.[32]

<u>International commodity study groups</u>

Study groups have been established for a large number of commodities. In the field of agricultural commodities, the FAO has been particularly active in establishing such bodies. The first task of a study group is to collect material on the commodity with which it deals, to prepare statistics and forecasts for production, export supply, international demand, price prospects, etc. The study groups also act as forums where exporter and importer representatives can meet to discuss common problems. Groups of this type are usually the first step towards reaching an International Commodity Agreement.

During recent years the <u>Cocoa</u> Study Group has been particularly active, and has prepared several drafts for an international agreement, the primary aim of which would be to stabilize price fluctuations. A UN Cocoa Conference, called in 1963 to consider a draft agreement, failed to reach consensus on account of divergent views between exporters and importers regarding minimum prices. The five major producer countries of the group then formed a Producer Alliance with the objective of stabilizing prices.[33] In more recent international meetings the main problem has been the division of costs for operating an agreement. These costs would include stock maintenance and, possibly also compensatory contributions to exporting countries.[34] Suggestions about division of the world market into two parts by price differentiation, as in the case of coffee, and about promotional activities, particularly in countries where cocoa consumption is still low and price and income elasticity likely to be high, have also been considered by the Cocoa Group.

World production of <u>olive oil</u> amounts to a little above 1 million tons, representing a total value of some $700 million. The entire production is located within the Mediterranean area, which also accounts for 95% of world consumption.[35] The olive trees supply bumper crops with a periodicity of 2 years. This 2-year cycle is not fully synchronized between the producing countries. Most of the olive oil is consumed internally within the producing countries, but when a meagre crop is experienced, a country will tend to substitute imported cheaper types of oil for olive oil consumption.

Consequently, countries with bumper crops have difficulties in finding outlets for their surplus.

An International Olive Council was established in 1958, but collaboration between its member countries has been confined to the exchange of information. Italy, the second largest producer and largest importer, has been unwilling to participate in price adjustment schemes in view of national agricultural considerations.

Proposals for international collaboration have included schemes for expansion of trade, to even out bumper and meagre year supplies between countries, and for the establishment of buffer stocks.

Among other important Commodity Study Groups, those for Grains other than wheat, for Cotton, Wool, Rubber, Citrus fruits, Lead and Zinc may be mentioned.

Notes and references to Chapter III

1) UNCTAD I, New York 1964, Proceedings, Vol. III, p. 516.

2) UNCTAD I, New York 1964, Proceedings, Vol. III, p. 518.

3) J. W. F. Rowe, Primary commodities in international trade, Cambridge 1965, p. 174.

4) The numerical facts from UNCTAD I, New York 1964, Proceedings, Vol. III, p. 50, 300 and 301.

5) UNCTAD I, New York 1964, Proceedings, Vol. III, p. 88 and 99.

6) J. W. F. Rowe, Primary commodities in international trade, Cambridge 1965, p. 175.

7) Economist, Nov. 2, 1968, p. 74.

8) UNCTAD I, New York 1964, Proceedings, Vol. III, p. 94, 99, 469.

9) J. W. F. Rowe, Primary commodities in international trade, Cambridge 1965, p. 170.

E

10) UNCTAD I, New York 1964, Proceedings, Vol. III, p. 137.

11) UNCTAD: Commodity problems and policies, TD/8/Suppl. 1, stencil, Nov. 14, 1967, p. 69.

12) UNCTAD I, New York 1964, Proceedings, Vol. III, p. 93 and Rowe, p. 173.

13) J. W. F. Rowe, Primary commodities in international trade, Cambridge 1965, p. 173.

14) The period of excess prices in 1964 and 1965 will be analyzed in greater detail in section VI. 3.

15) FAO Monthly Bulletin, May 1966, p. 9.

16) UNCTAD I, New York 1964, Proceedings, Vol. III, p. 100 and 506.

17) UNCTAD I, New York 1964, Proceedings, Vol. III, p. 91 and 144, and Rowe, p. 163-169.

18) P. 165

19) UNCTAD I, New York 1964, Proceedings, Vol. III, p. 506.

20) UNCTAD I, New York 1964, Proceedings, Vol. III, p. 144 and Rowe, p. 167.

21) FAO Commodity Review, 1968.

22) L. R. Brown, 'The Agricultural Revolution in Asia', Foreign Affairs, July 1968.

23) UN Statistical Yearbook 1965, p. 120.

24) J. W. F. Rowe, Primary commodities in international trade, Cambridge 1965, p. 179.

25) J. W. F. Rowe, Primary commodities in international trade, Cambridge 1965, p. 180.

26) UNCTAD I, New York 1964, Proceedings, Vol. III, p. 145.

27) Commodity Yearbook 1964, New York, p. 23.

28) FAO Monthly Bulletin, October 1965, p. 9.

29) FAO Monthly Bulletin, March 1966, p. 4.

30) Commodity Yearbook 1964, New York, p. 24.

31) UNCTAD I, New York 1964, Proceedings, Vol. III, p. 89, 314.

32)   P.Bohm, <u>Pricing of Copper</u>, Stockholm 1966, p.5.

33)   UNCTAD I, New York 1964, Proceedings, Vol.III, p.313.

34)   FAO Monthly Bulletin, March 1966, article by T.Lehti.

35)   FAO Monthly Bulletin, March 1965.

IV WHY EXPORT RESTRICTIONS DON'T SUCCEED

IV.1 <u>The monopoly effects of export restrictions</u>

The operation of international export restriction schemes usually
implies the fixing of an "acceptable" price, and adjusting output
downwards, if the price moves below the target value. This policy
is in fact the same as that of a monopolist, and consequently the
two monopoly conditions must be fulfilled if the scheme is to be
successful, namely:

1. Production decisions should be reached in collusion
    between all the production units, and

2. There must not be any close substitute for the
    commodity concerned.

A price-fixing and supply-adjusting scheme of this type will not
necessarily lead to a stabilization of export revenue for the countries participating. As has been shown in section I.3, the effects
on revenue will depend on the shifts in and elasticities of the
demand and supply schedules.

Let us study the effects of an export restriction scheme under the
simplifying assumption of steady demand and supply schedules,
which are known to producers. Figure IV.1 depicts the world
supply and demand conditions, where supply has been obtained by
the lateral addition of the individual producers' supply curves.
With no collusion agreement, Q_3 will be supplied at the price of P_1.
According to well-known monopoly theory, the producers' profits
would be maximized by reducing output to Q_1, and charging the
price of P_2. Here, however, comes the first complication. By a
reduction of output, factors of production will be released. In a
diversified and developed economy these factors are likely to find
an alternative employment at or close to the wage level at which
they were remunerated earlier. In an underdeveloped economy,
their alternative cost is smaller, and could even be as low as zero.
The reason why, in the case of labor, wages are nevertheless far

above zero, is naturally that there is a minimum subsistence wage, below which labor cannot be employed. If the government has to cater for the unemployed, we may well face a situation, where the private cost of additional employment, reflected in the S-curve in Figure IV.1 is higher than the corresponding social cost. The social supply curve could therefore be situated much below the private one.

This helps in explaining the common tendency in commodity discussion to focus attention on maximization of revenue rather than profit. Revenue will be maximized at output Q_2, where the marginal revenue equals zero, and the price elasticity of demand amounts to 1. A policy aiming at this level of output would be justified if the social cost of factors in the relevant range is at or close to zero. Even if unemployment is created by reduction of output from Q_3 to Q_2, transfers to the unemployed could make everybody better off. A further output restriction to Q_1 would not be rational in these circumstances, because total revenue decreases for outputs below Q_2. After noting this problem, let us, however, assume in the continued exposition that there is no divergence between the social and private marginal costs, and proceed further in our analysis.

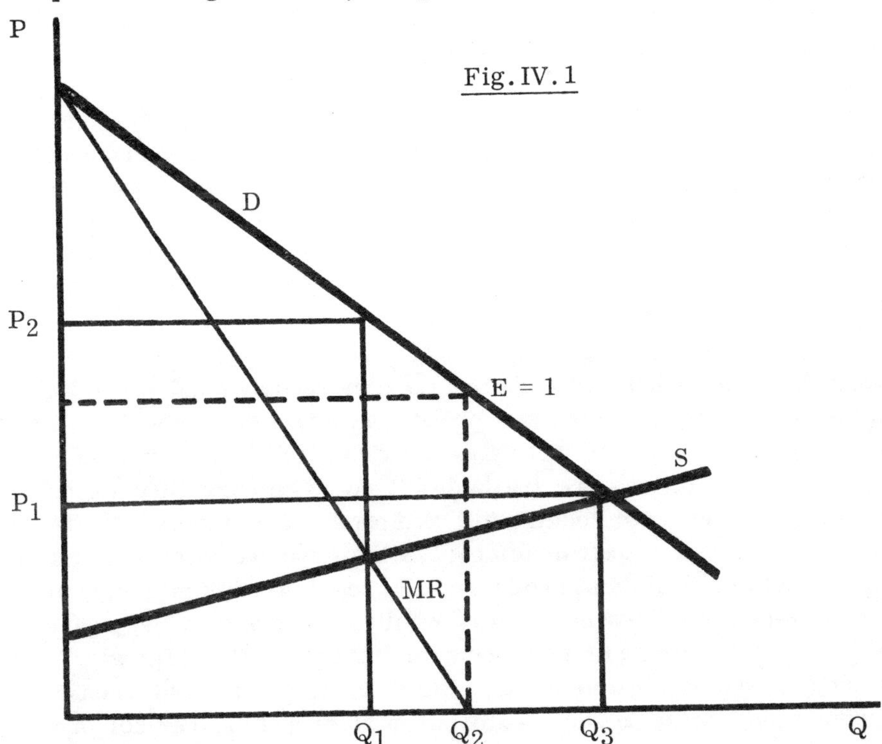

The export restriction scheme can be likened to a multiplant monopoly, where the various plants correspond to the producing countries which participate. The conditions for profit maximization now necessitate that each country's marginal production cost is equalized. In Figure IV.2 the supply schedules for the three participating countries are marked S_1, S_2 and S_3 respectively, adding up to a total supply schedule, marked S_T. Profit maximization requires production of Q_T, with country 2 supplying Q_1, country 3 supplying Q_2, and country 1 discontinuing production altogether. The proof is easy to provide. An increase of production by one unit in any country will cost more than the corresponding reduction of one unit in another. Thus, costs at the margin must be equal in all countries for profit maximization. [1]

In the real world conditions, the situation will not be as simple as this analysis might suggest. First of all there is the uncertainty of the market demand conditions. Each participant in the export restriction may have his own appraisal of the responsiveness of the market demand to prices, and a corresponding recommendation on the optimal total output. Second, there is the problem of exchange rates. If these have been established without regard to international competitiveness, the above conditions for profit maximization will not hold. Suppose that overvaluation of the currency in country 1 is the explanation of its high production costs when measured in terms of dollars: a correction of this overvaluation will lower the supply curve of country 1, and profit maximization will consequently require a different set of quantities supplied from each of the three countries. The lack of norms for what is to be regarded as currency over- or undervaluation therefore further weakens the ground for the definiteness of the analytical profit maximization argument, presented above.

Apart from this vagueness, there is one more important reason why, in the real world, monopolistic profit maximization is not likely to be reached. This is the fact that even if uniquely determined cost and demand conditions are available, it would be very difficult to convince the high cost country to leave production entirely, or to persuade the others to transfer part of their export revenue so as to compensate the high cost producer. To reach maximum monopoly profits, each participating country would have to accept the production quota determined by some central authority. On political grounds it seems improbable that the national governments concerned would agree to such "external interference". The compromise agreement likely to be reached will instead be to maximize total profits subject to the restraint that each country maintains its share of earlier total sales. The reduction of monopoly profits, which will follow from the adoption of historical shares, is the price which must be paid for maintenance of independence and decentralized decision-making. That the profits of this "collective monopoly" will be smaller than in a single monopoly will be due to two reasons. First, the costs for a given output in a collective monopoly based on historical shares will be higher than in a single monopoly. This is because a single monopoly, unlike a collective one, can maintain higher efficiency by concentrating its production in the most efficiently producing countries, and by eliminating duplication in its administrative and distributive machinery. Second, the collective monopoly may not adopt the most profitable market offer, because the differing marginal costs in the various countries will make it difficult to determine the profit-maximizing total output. [2]

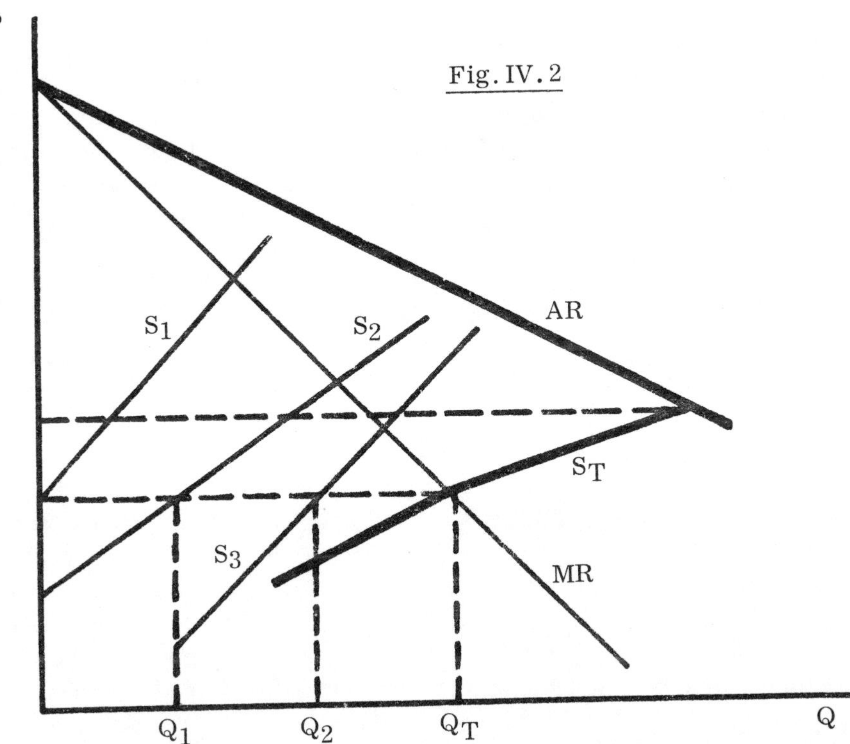

In a world of national political ambitions, uncertain demand conditions, and artificial exchange rates which can only be upheld with the help of import quotas and other trade barriers, the adoption of

64

historical quotas in export restriction schemes may appear as the most reasonable of the available and acceptable choices. Without strong simplifications it is not even possible to provide a definite proof that a different export restriction policy would be economically more efficient.

IV.2 Operating problems at the national level

An individual country which takes part in an export restriction scheme will face the problem of how to diminish exports of the commodity concerned by the proportion required. With the heavy public involvement in commodity export activities, the government of the country will in most cases be responsible for carrying through the restriction measures. Several methods are possible.

If the objective of the scheme is to shield the prices from a temporary demand fall, there may be an understanding among the participating countries that export restrictions will last for a short period only. In this situation, the best policy for the government may be to leave production undisturbed, and to build up national stocks, which could be sold out when demand increases and the restriction is discontinued. If, on the other hand, restriction is expected to become a lasting feature, more permanent measures are required.

The first possible policy for the government could be to promote an increase of internal consumption or use of the commodity. This policy requires that an internal demand can be created without too great difficulties. It would hardly be feasible with copper in under-developed economies like Chile or Zambia. It could, on the other hand, well be suitable for rice, tea, coffee and cocoa in the countries where these commodities are produced. Promotion of internal consumption could be achieved by reduction of consumption taxes or by the introduction of consumer subsidies. Increments of internal use could be a suitable policy objective where internal processing is feasible, and the processed product is not affected by the restriction. The government might promote the establishment of chocolate factories or processing plants for instant coffee, in which the unexportable surplus of the commodity could be used. One problem with this policy is that effective duties on processed goods are prohibitively high in most developed markets; another is that if primary producing countries generally were to take up processing for exports, international prices for the processed commodity would tend to deteriorate.

A stage may come when, in spite of other efforts, it becomes
necessary to restrict production. The government's choice then
appears to be between two principal measures. It can either use
taxation of output or some of the inputs required in production, or
else it may in some way ration the permission to produce.[3)] The
effects are similar to those of excise taxes versus rationing, to
reduce consumption of a scarce commodity.[4)] Let us discuss
these effects from the point of view of economic efficiency.

A tax will drive high-cost producers out of production, while a
rationing scheme will usually have a tendency to conserve prevailing
production patterns. Production taxation will therefore lead to
lower overall production costs, and therefore it seems preferable to
rationing. Connected with economic efficiency is the question:
which policy will lead to a smoother reallocation of factors into
alternative lines of production? No definite statement can be made
here. If low production costs depend on broader knowledge and
higher managerial skill, such as are to be found among the large-
scale producers, one could perhaps argue that this category of
entrepreneurs is more adaptable, and that therefore a rationing
policy, hitting them relatively harder than taxation, would lead to
a smoother reallocation of factors to production of other goods.
This line of reasoning, which lets the large producers carry a
higher burden of the restriction scheme, would also seem preferable
on social equity grounds.

A dynamic consideration in favor of taxation arises from the likely
behavior among producers if their income is assured by the allot-
ment of rations combined with high and stable prices. The production sector will then lack incentives to innovate and rationalize. In
the absence of rationing, all producers must be constantly on the
alert against competition from new-comers or from improved
production methods, and the probability is that in course of time
this will lead to increased efficiency in production.

Another argument concerns the income-redistributive effects of
rationing. Even if rationing is applied, increased production taxes
would be required if the government wants to prevent the income
redistribution favoring producers, that is caused by increased
international prices. In the absence of additional taxes, a ration to
produce the commodity concerned will carry with it a remuneration
similar to Ricardo's land rent. Once taxes are increased to the
level where no rents accrue to the ration-holders, e.g. when supply

and demand for rations are equalized, there is no longer any necessity to apply rationing. Unless the government desires to shift the income distribution in favor of producers, taxation seems the superior of the two methods.

It is obvious that in the distorted and inflexible markets of an under-developed economy, any general statements of the type presented above, must be surrounded by a great amount of caution. With the weak administrative systems in u-countries, it may be somewhat difficult to enforce a strict rationing system in the face of a very remunerative production, resulting from the high international prices. Checking production by taxation also has its problems, but those seem easier to manage, especially if tax is applied at the time of exportation. On the whole, therefore, there appears more to be said for production or export taxes than for a system of rationing, to curb the production of a commodity.

Restrictions will be easier to accomplish for commodities whose production requires little fixed capital. Little capital loss needs to be realized if the output of rice, wheat or cotton is to be reduced from season to season. The economic strain on producers will be heavier, and restriction measures more difficult for capital-intensive commodities like underground minerals or tree crops, e.g. coffee and cocoa. It will be advantageous to producers to continue production as long as their receipts carry a contribution to fixed costs over and above variable costs. The latter could well be fairly insignificant. In some types of mining, production must be maintained continuously, and a mine, once closed, cannot be re-opened without substantial costs. Thus, very heavy taxation would be required to reduce production of capital-intensive commodities. Investment in tree crops depreciates slowly; the life of rubber, tea, coffee and coconut trees stretches over several decades. The adjustment process, therefore, will be both painful and long-drawn-out. In the case of tea and rubber, production is more easily regulated in the short run by variations in plucking of leaves and tapping. Thus, short-period restrictions for these commodities are relatively easier to carry out.

Last among the internal problems to be taken up here is how strictly the government of a u-country will be prepared to enforce production restriction. On the one hand, very attractive prices seem to be almost within reach. On the other is the cumbersome problem of reconstructing the economy and providing new employment for large numbers of workers. Facing this situation, the government could decide to maintain production and build stocks, although it knows that over a longer period such a policy will be untenable. At least three explanations of this choice of policy can be thought of: first, the unwillingness or inability to tackle the unemployment problems; secondly, the fact that governments in many u-countries are fairly short-lived - the current government could be coldly calculating that it will no longer be in power when the stockholding becomes too burdensome; and thirdly, a sizeable stock is an efficient pressure on the partners to the agreement to increase the country's export quota. The stock could even be used as a threat to break the agreement, unless a more generous quota is received. That such policies do not increase the stability of export restriction agreements hardly needs to be pointed out.

IV.3 <u>Operating problems, international</u>

To reach an agreement requires complicated negotiations, and a good deal of compromising between the parties. In spite of the aggregate advantages which could be reaped, it is difficult or even impossible to persuade all current and potential producers to join. The unwillingness may be due to a multiplicity of reasons. A country can, for instance, hesitate because of the economic disturbances which it will have to face internally. Alternatively, a producing country could belong to a different political camp, and perhaps not even be invited to participate in the agreement. There has for example not been any serious consideration as to whether to include Mainland China in the tin agreement. A related reason for limited incentives to join could be if an exporting country already has an assured export market at favorable prices within an existing economic block. Examples of such situations are easy to provide from the Commonwealth preference system, the Franc Zone arrangements or the US preferential quota imports of some commodities from selected countries. It would probably also be more difficult to persuade a potential producer country with no current output to join. For such a country there are no immediate economic advantages from participating, to balance against the restriction of freedom which participation implies.

Unless the agreement succeeds in assembling all or practically all current and potential producers of significance, there will be grave risks of breakdown over a longer period. The price increase which is established at a cost to the parties in the agreement, will favor production expansion in non-participating producing countries, and an initiation of production in countries which were potential producers only. The profit-maximizing sales policy for the non-participants will then be to offer the commodity at prices just below those established by the agreement. By doing this, they will succeed in selling all their production first. If the output of th⌐ non-participants constitutes only a small proportion of total demand at the fixed price, the participants in the agreement may be content with the remaining sales which they are able to make.[5] But if outside production is sizeable or grows at fast rates, the policies of the agreement will soon have to be reconsidered. Either the outsiders should be induced to join, or the pricing policies should be changed, or else a multilateral contract, with importer obligations to buy from restricting exporters only, will somehow have to be established. If none of these measures is undertaken, the agreement runs a serious risk of falling apart. Even when all producers participate, a policy of excessively high prices may easily lead to efforts to develop synthetic substitutes to the natural commodity. The effects will be the same as those of natural outsider production.

While the discussion with regard to non-participation is related to the problems of supply increases, we now turn to the opposite, namely demand reactions caused by the high price level. In the beginning of this chapter we stated that a condition for the establishment of an export restriction scheme is the absence of close substitutes. Now it is necessary to look a little closer at the problem of substitution, and in particular at its effect over slightly longer time intervals.

Long-term substitution is extremely difficult to estimate or predict, but the likelihood is that it is much higher than its short-term counterpart. In terms of supply-demand analysis, this would mean that the long-term demand schedule is more elastic than its short-term correspondent at each price. Graphically the argument could be presented as in Figure IV.3 where, with S representing the supply schedule which remains invariant over a period of time, and AR_S and MR_S being the short-run revenue schedules, profit-maximizing export restriction pushes price up to P_2 by a reduction of supply from Q_4 to Q_2. After all adaptations on the demand side, however, the quantity demanded at price P_2 will prove to be not Q_2 but Q_1. Apparently substitution in the long run was much higher than in the short run. We can now draw the AR_L schedule, and from it price P_1, much below P_2, and quantity Q_3 appear to be the ones through which the producing side maximizes its profits.

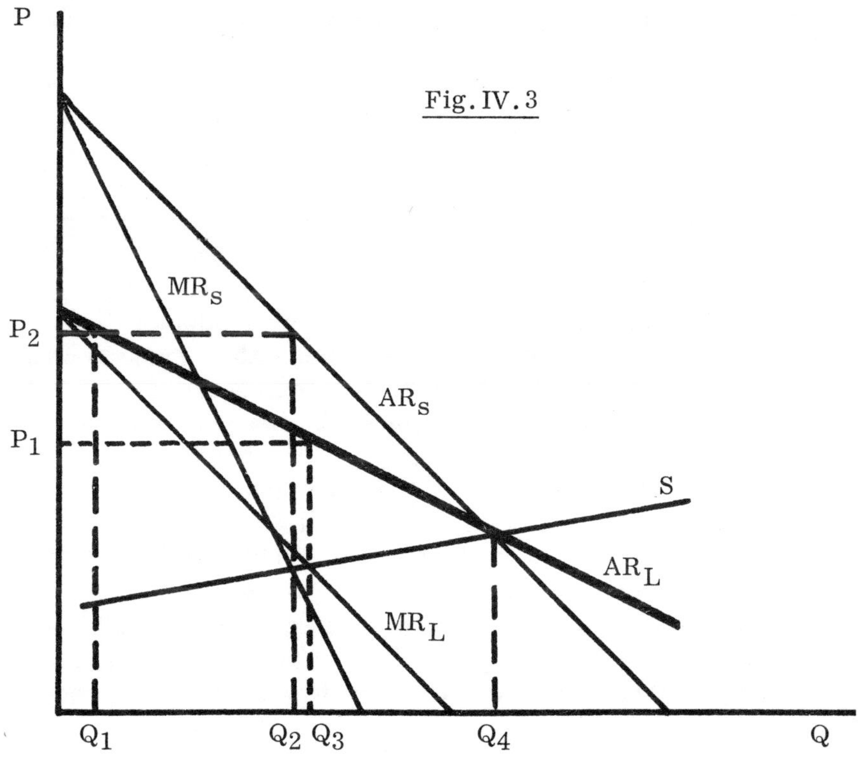

How does one explain the difference between short-run and long-run substitution? Possibly, a line of reasoning such as that which follows, taking coffee as an example, could be used. The short-run demand curve measures the immediate transfer of consumption to close substitutes like tea or chocolate. (We disregard the income effects of a price change.) Consumers are, on the other hand, not as quick in their transfer of consumption habits from coffee to more distant substitutes. It takes a longer time to reconsider wider consumption choices on the basis of the new relative price pattern. New habits take time to develop. Eventually, the consumption gain will perhaps not be in tea but in beer or candies. An additional dimension is introduced by the constant generation change. Habitual coffee-drinkers may stick to their consumption irrespective of prices; but they will gradually be replaced by new generations, who form all their habits on the basis of current conditions. In the end everything can be a substitute for coffee. A practically identical argument could be used to explain the higher long-run price elasticities of demand for almost any commodity, agricultural as well as mineral.

A number of investigations have been undertaken to calculate the
increase in the tropical commodity trade of u-countries, which
would result from a consumer price decrease through the abolition
of price-raising trade barriers in i-countries. Invariantly these
calculations result in insignificant increases in trade.

> "For non-competing commodities, removal of existing Northern
> duties and internal taxes would have only a modest effect.
> Taxes on coffee, tea, cocoa, tin and spices are a nuisance to
> LDC's, but they do not greatly affect consumption of these
> commodities, because demand is so inelastic. Tinbergen has
> estimated that removal of duties and fiscal charges on coffee,
> tea and bananas in 1959 would have increased Atlantic Com-
> munity imports of those products by $ 64 million, about 2.5%
> of the value of world trade in these commodities. A similar
> estimate by GATT for 1961, worked out to about $ 100-130
> million for coffee, cocoa and bananas worldwide. An FAO
> projection made in 1962, adding cocoa and citrus fruits to the
> list of crops, emerged with a trade effect of $ 180 million for
> Europe (the US does not tax imports of these products), or
> about 4% of the projected 1970 value of world trade in these
> crops."[6]

Could it be that what is considered in these calculations is the change
caused by short-run substitution, sometimes extended over longer
periods, but that they fail to take account of the dynamic long-run
substitution effects, and that if the latter were assessed, much
higher figures for the trade increase would be obtained?

A problem common to all commodity agreements, but elegantly
obviated in the general compensatory finance schemes, is the difficulty of correct estimation of the equilibrium price, supply and
demand trends. The further the administered price deviates from
that which would equilibrate the market in the absence of restrictions, the stronger will be the tensions on the agreement, and the
larger will be the risks for an eventual break of the whole
arrangement.

The price determination in an unregulated market is sensitive to
the constant dynamic changes which take place due to, for instance,
changed consumption habits, improvement of productivity in production, discovery of new mineral resources and so on, and the market
process will indicate more or less perfectly the consecutive equili-

brium price levels. The authority which administers a restriction scheme, will be in a much less certain position, when trying to estimate the effects of dynamic change. Without full-scale market experiments, which are not feasible in practice, the track of the equilibrium price is almost certain to be lost.

IV.1 <u>Conclusions</u>

It should be clear from the arguments in the first section in this chapter that an export restriction agreement can be profitable, in some cases highly so, for participating (and even more for non-participating) countries. What then is the practical experience of export restrictions? Soon after the first world war, export restriction schemes were introduced for several commodities, e.g. sugar, copper and rubber. They were quite successful in temporarily raising prices. Over the years, the experience of some of them emphasize what has been pointed out above about outsider production. In the case of rubber, for instance, emergence of new, unregulated production in what is now Indonesia, broke the scheme already in 1928. The violent demand decrease in the crisis of 1930 broke whatever restriction schemes which had succeeded to avoid other problems. New restrictions were attempted with varying success in the 1930's for copper, rubber, tea and sugar. Greater care was now taken to include all actual and potential producers. The outbreak of the second world war terminated all the schemes.[7] The history after 1945 has been given in detail in the previous chapter.

What comes out is that for some years an export restriction agreement can be very successful in raising prices and increasing earnings. With time, however, as touch is more and more lost with equilibrium, the vulnerability of the agreement to external shocks of any kind will gradually grow. When the break eventually comes, it may have very disruptive effects on the industry, with grave balance of payments problems for the exporting countries. Some of the damage could even be irreversible, for example in the case of synthetic developments.

Are then export restrictions on the whole economically disadvantageous to u-countries? Not necessarily so. Two considerations must be taken up before reaching a final conclusion. The first is that much more varied experience is available about ordinary industrial monopolies, from which some relevant deductions could be made. Successful monopolies usually have a highly centralized decision-making machinery, and adopt a flexible approach in their pricing policies, whenever they sense a risk of competition by new entrants or by substitute products. An improvement of these two features in international export restriction agreements would certainly go a long way to increase their stability.

The second consideration is that u-countries could need increased revenue now, to give a push to their development efforts and to the diversification of their economies. Thus, if export restriction increases the earnings of a country for several years, and the increment is successfully used to make it less dependent on the commodity concerned, then it may well be worth-while to introduce restriction measures, even if a crash is eventually expected.

Notes and references to Chapter IV

1) For an algebraic proof see Cohen-Cyert, Theory of the Firm, New Jersey, 1965, p.235-236.

2) See also T.Scitovsky, Welfare and competition, London, 1952, chapter 17.

3) Taxation or rationing of exports instead of production is fully feasible where internal use of the commodity is insignificant.

4) For a detailed account of these effects, see J.Tobin, 'A Survey of the Theory of Rationing', Econometrica, Oct.1952.

5) For a formal analysis of the likely behavior in this situation, see the discussion on the "dominant firm" in Cohen-Cyert, Theory of the Firm, New Jersey, 1965, p.241-242.

6) J.Pincus, Trade, Aid and Development, New York, 1967, p.261.

7) For a closer analysis of the inter-war commodity agreements see J.W.F.Rowe, Primary Commodity in International Trade, Cambridge 1965, part IV.

V CAN MULTILATERAL CONTRACTS STRENGTHEN EXPORT RESTRICTION SCHEMES?

V.1 Definitions

A multilateral contract is an agreement between several producing and consuming countries about the volume and/or price in the exchange of a commodity. In this respect it carries a great similarity to the long-term bilateral contracts between u-countries and the Socialist block, briefly discussed in chapter II. Little practical experience is available on the working of multilateral contracts. The wheat agreement has hardly functioned as intended. Rather, prices have been administered by a stock-holding policy of the two North-American producers. The coffee agreement, which is a combination of a multilateral contract and an export restriction scheme, is still too new to allow definite conclusions.

The importer obligations, which constitute the significant new feature in multilateral contracts, could in a sense be described as an extension of a producers' export restriction agreement. These obligations can take a multiplicity of forms. They can for instance consist of an undertaking by the importing countries to buy all their needs exclusively from exporting members. Alternatively, the importing countries can promise to buy specific quantities from member countries. Various clauses can be contained in the contract regarding the prices at which transactions should be made, as well as about quantities sold outside the multilateral agreement. A number of further provisions can be added to suit the features of a particular commodity, or to be convenient to the importers or exporters. Thus the multilateral contract is not at all as strictly defined as export restrictions or buffer stock measures for commodity market regulation. It follows that it is hardly possible to analyze multilateral contracts as such. Their implications will be entirely dependent on the form given to each specific agreement. In view of this, we propose to look first at some few points of a more general nature, which will probably turn up in most multilateral agreements. Subsequently we will look a little closer at the

F

effects of some additional measures undertaken by the importers within a multilateral contract for the specific benefit of exporting countries. To reduce the level of abstraction, these will be studied in the context of the coffee agreement.

V.2 <u>Operating problems</u>

The active importer participation adds strength and stability to a multilateral agreement, but simultaneously it makes the initial negotiations much more difficult. While both the exporting and importing side are likely to be interested in stability of prices and of volume supplied, their interests will diverge with regard to the price level at which transactions should take place. The price level, or sometimes the price range is determined by a bargaining process between exporters and importers. The outcome will depend, inter alia, on the strength of the two parties. The position of the exporting countries will be weakened if they are many and have no uniform approach to the export policy to be bargained for. An existing agreement among exporters regarding export restrictions or other measures to regulate the flow of the commodity will improve their position. The monopolistic pressure of the exporting side will be further strengthened if the commodity lacks close substitutes and is indispensable in consumption or in important production processes in the importing countries. If, on the other hand, the commodity is easily replaceable, then the importing countries will be able to use the threat of substitutes as an argument to keep prices down. Sizeable stocks or projections indicating a fast expansion of production without a corresponding increase in use will also have price dampening effects in the bargaining process.

A multilateral contract which ensures export markets at predetermined prices for a major share of the producing countries' output, will certainly be of great advantage to exporting participants. By making their export revenue much more certain, it will facilitate their long-term development planning. The assurance of supply over a longer period at predictable prices should also be an advantage to the importing countries.

Rather than being dictated by economic arguments, the importer obligations which favor exporting countries, often seem to be motivated by political reasoning. So long as, for political reasons, they find it advantageous, importing countries will stick to their obligations, even when they could get more advantageous terms in an unregulated market, or outside the agreement. With a sudden political change, however, their willingness to support can totally disappear. This inherent political instability of multilateral contracts, naturally reduces their value to exporting members, whose economies are heavily dependent on the commodity concerned.

A multilateral contract is usually more flexible than simple export restriction in the sense that it does not require the participation of all producers. Agreement can be reached between selected importing and exporting countries without specific regard to production in non-member countries. With time, when the agreement is to be renegotiated, the developments of world supply and world consumption, will nevertheless play a certain role for the determination of prices and volumes in the renewed agreement.

Aside from trade on the terms of the multilateral contract, free market transactions of the following type are possible:

1. From member exporters to member importers
2. From member exporters to non-member importers
3. From non-member exporters to member importers
4. From non-member exporters to non-member importers.

Transactions in category 1 and 2 presuppose that the agreement does not stipulate that total members' exports be covered by the agreement, and similarly for categories 1 and 3 with regard to members' imports. As prices within the agreement are determined by a bargaining process, and may deviate from what they would be in market equilibrium, the question now arises, to what extent the free market prices can be a reliable guide of what the equilibrium price would be in the absence of any agreement. The ability to use free market prices in this way is sometimes claimed to be an advantage of multilateral contracts over other commodity arrangement tools. [1)] It appears that as a rule the free market price cannot be assigned this indicative role, whenever it deviates from the regulated price. The reason is that a multilateral contract, covering a sizeable share of the total market, will distort the free market conditions. Suppose that a major exporter has been excluded from the agreement, while all substantial importing countries consent to cover their imports from exporter members. The lack of market outlets outside the agreement will result in a much more severe depression of the free market price than in the absence of the multi-

lateral contract. Free market prices will be much above the
equilibrium level in the opposite case, if the supply to a non-member
importing country is restricted through the operations of the agreement. The multilateral contract can thus destabilize prices in the
free market. The loss of touch with equilibrium prices will create
problems similar to those experienced in export restriction schemes.

Price destabilization in the free market will occur even if all major
exporters and importers participate. This is due to the income
effect on importers from the non-equilibrium prices of the agreement. If the contract price falls below that of the free market, the
real income will rise in the importing countries, whereby demand
on the free market increases and results in a higher free price than
in the absence of any agreement. The opposite will hold if the
contract price lies below the free market level.[2)] For most commodities, however, this effect is not likely to be very important in
view of the limited weight of each commodity in the budgets of the
consumers.

It may be the purpose of the agreement to secure prices above
equilibrium level to a group of u-countries. Initial negotiations will
then constitute less of a problem. Such an agreement can be seen
as a measure by the participating i-countries, to assist the u-
countries to arrange an export restriction scheme. A number of the
difficulties discussed in connection with export restrictions will now
be experienced. A simple enumeration seems to be sufficient here.
The reader interested in the background analysis is referred back to
chapter IV. Thus there will be the difficulties in holding back production, so as to prevent it from rising in response to the advantageous prices. Restriction can easily lead to conservation of
production patterns with the inefficiencies in resource allocation
which are likely to arise therefrom. There will also be the problem
of reaching an agreement on export quota distribution between the
participating exporter countries. Substitution into alternative commodities or into synthetics will certainly be a problem, although its
effects in the short run could be neutralized by the importer obligations to buy. A problem specific to multilateral contracts is that
they may effectively prevent the emergence of more efficient production in countries which do not participate in the agreement. From a
world-wide point of view the result will be a lower production
efficiency than in the absence of the contract.

V.3 Some additional importer engagements

We have selected the coffee agreement as the basis of reference in
the following discussion of some further measures aimed at assisting
the exporting countries within a multilateral contract. The conclusions apply equally well to other commodities, although for those
with substitutes produced in i-countries, care would have to be taken
to frame the assistance measures so that only the products origina-
ting in u-countries could benefit.

The coffee agreement obliges participating importers to purchase
all their coffee from member exporters. Prices are to be maintained by export quota restrictions around the level which prevailed
in 1962, which, judging from export quota quarrels and expanding
production, is probably a very remunerative level, well above the
unregulated market equilibrium. In chapter III we have taken up
some of the problems experienced in the coffee agreement. Both
in chapter III and in the previous section of this chapter we have
discussed the advantage accruing to exporters from the effective
exclusion of outsider producers through a multilateral contract like
the one for coffee. But in current commodity discussion, the
impression is sometimes given that further gains accrue to exporters from the importer participation in multilateral agreements.
Disregarding the effects on outsider production, the question to be
taken up now could be phrased: Do exporting participants derive
any additional economic advantage from a multilateral agreement
like the one for coffee, in comparison with what could be achieved
from a simple export restriction scheme?

The importing countries' demand for coffee depends on the demand
patterns of individual consuming units, and are directly related to
the prices charged from consumers. In the coffee agreement the
importing countries' obligation is limited to the condition that all
their purchases be made from member exporters. Importers are
however not obliged to undertake any measures to increase the
internal demand. The maintenance of prices above the intersection
of the unregulated demand and supply schedules is therefore attained
entirely by the export-restricting actions of the exporting side.
The net result of the coffee agreement will be equal to a simple
export restriction scheme, with prices possibly below the monopolistic profit maximum level, due to the importer influence in the
bargaining process.

78

To create further advantages to exporting countries in the agreement, the importer governments would have to increase the
domestic demand in some way. This could be done by decreasing
consumption taxes on coffee, introduction of coffee subsidies, or by
sales promotional campaigns paid by the importing governments.
(For a commodity like coffee without close substitutes produced in
the importing country, a sales tax and an import duty will have the
same effect. In the whole argument below, introduction of consumption subsidies will have effects equal to the abolition of taxes.) Let
us now analyze the effects of consumption taxes in importing countries on the profits of the exporting countries. For simplicity, the
following analysis is restricted to one exporting and one importing
country only. Without any change in the conclusions, the analysis
could be generalized to several countries.

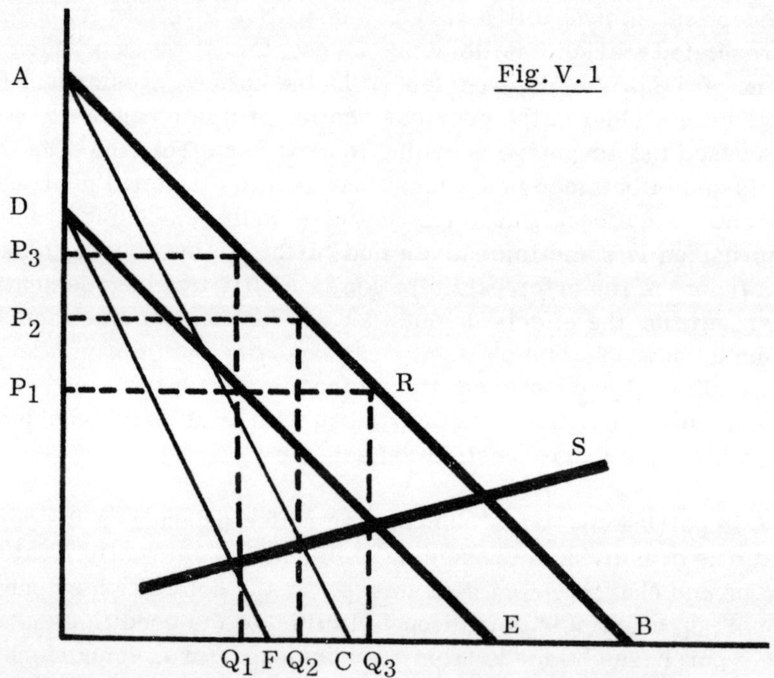

In Figure V. 1, AB is the original demand schedule, while DE is
demand after imposition of a unit tax. [3] With export restriction as
in the coffee agreement, exports are optimally reduced to Q_1,
prices received by the exporting country will be P_1, while consumers
in the importing country will pay P_3. The importer country may
wish to assist the exporter by abolishing the unit tax. The exporter's
profit-maximizing policy would now be to sell Q_2 at price P_2, which

is more advantageous than his position before the abolition of the
unit tax. (On condition that the elasticity of supply is non-negative.)
The importer government might however agree to discontinue the
tax only on condition that the export price P_1 is maintained.   The
profit-maximizing policy will now be to extend exports up to Q_3.
where the supply curve intersects the new kinked marginal revenue
curve P_1RQ_3.   Whether, on balance, this new position will be better
or worse for the exporters than the positions P_2Q_2 or P_1Q_1 will
depend on the elasticity of the supply curve.   The lower the supply
elasticity, the less advantage will the exporting country derive from
production expansion at given prices.

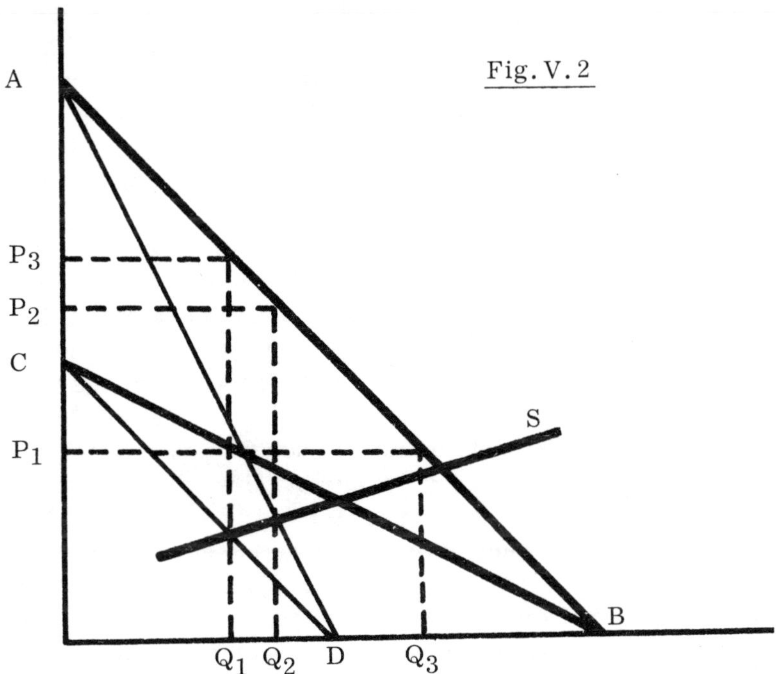

Fig. V. 2

The argument will be similar, if the importing country operates an
ad valorem tax on the internal sales of coffee. In Figure V.2, AB
is the demand schedule without tax, CB the decreased demand due
to the ad valorem tax. With the tax, producers' optimal exports
would be Q_1. Prices received by the exporting country would then
amount to P_1, and prices paid by consumers in the importing
country would be P_3. Maximization of profits by the exporting side,
when the tax is abolished, will expand production to Q_2, while
exporters' and consumers' prices are equalized at P_2. This again
will be more advantageous to the exporting country (again assuming
a positively sloping supply curve). Whether an expansion of exports,

while maintaining the export price P_1 is advantageous to exporters, will also now depend on the elasticity of the supply curve.

We may further ask, with reference to both unit and ad valorem tax, if, from the exporters' point of view, an abolition of taxes would be preferable to a policy where the taxes are maintained, but the whole tax revenue is remitted to the exporting country. It is apparent that this is a matter of complete indifference to the exporters. Assuming that, while the tax is maintained, the average revenue to exporting countries from production Q_1 is increased from P_1 to P_3 through an international transfer of the total tax revenues, the relevant demand schedule to producers will now be AB, and profit maximization will require a production increase to Q_2 - which will result in a total revenue, including tax transfers, equal to that of profit maximization in the absence of taxes. On the importing side the tax will have two effects. First, it will redistribute income and secondly, it will carry some administrative costs.

The above exercises disregard the dynamic influences and the long-run effects of tax changes, some of which could be irreversible. Despite their simplification, the exercises point to a few reasonable conclusions. The first is that, apart from keeping off outsider production, a multilateral contract in itself usually offers no advantage to producing countries over and above what can be achieved by a simple export restriction scheme. Secondly, an abolition of taxes or duties on a commodity like coffee will be profitable to both exporters (higher profits) and to consumers (lower prices), while the government of the importing country will lose the tax revenue. Thirdly, an abolition of taxes along with forced maintenance of prices received by the exporting country can be both advantageous and disadvantageous to the exporting country, depending on the price elasticity of supply. Fourthly, tax abolition or a scheme to transfer the tax revenue to the exporting country will result in an equal total revenue to the exporters.

The deduction to be made from the whole argument is that measures undertaken by importing countries to assist the exporting countries (abolition of taxes, transfer of tax revenues or introduction of subsidies on the imported commodity) will amount to a levy on the taxpayers or consumers of the importing country. It seems that greater objectivity could be achieved in the disbursement of the revenue of such levies, by disconnecting their distribution from commodity export considerations and instead applying some criteria of general assistance needs.

References and notes to Chapter V

1) See for instance A. MacBean, Export Instability and Economic Development, London 1966, p. 276.

2) See H. G. Johnson, 'The Destabilizing Effects of Intern. Commodity Agreements on the Prices of Primary Products', Economic Journal, Sept. 1950, p. 626.

3) The argument used here and in what follows about ad valorem tax, is an adaptation of the analysis of the effects of internal taxes on production decisions in Musgrave, Theory of Public Finance, Tokyo 1959, chapter 13. The reader may also refer to that text for a general algebraic exposition of the problems.

VI INTERNATIONAL BUFFER STOCKS:
AN EXPENSIVE STABILIZATION METHOD

The discussion in this chapter will be limited to international buffer stocks. Stabilization through buffers at the national level has been attempted frequently, with both stocks and funds and with governments as well as producers' associations as operators of the schemes. These activities fall outside our scope, and will not be taken up here.

Our discussion will be simplified by the assumption that the supply curves of individual countries giving the quantities offered for exports, reflect the social marginal costs of production (see discussion around Fig. IV.1 in chapter IV). We shall first discuss some difficulties, including the high costs of operating international buffer schemes, and then scrutinize the effects of international buffer stocks on the export revenue stabilization and export revenue changes in producing countries, under varying assumptions regarding supply and demand reactions. Further on we propose to have a closer look at the tin agreement, and to attempt a first approximation of the resources which would have been needed to ensure the objectives of the scheme during a particular period. Finally, we will discuss the somewhat utopic commodity currency proposal brought out by Hart, Kaldor and Tinbergen.

VI.1   Operating problems

As compared with export restriction schemes, buffer stocks are a much more flexible instrument. It is not necessary that all producers participate. Although this was not the intention of the international wheat agreement, the international wheat market was in fact regulated during the late 1950's by a bilateral US-Canadian buffer stock. Buffer schemes do not require any circumscribing of the functioning of the market mechanism, as is the case in a multilateral contract and in an export restriction agreement. The operator of the buffer stock behaves like an ordinary seller and buyer in the market, albeit a very sizeable one.

Unlike the tools for commodity arrangements considered in earlier
chapters, buffer schemes are unsuitable for price pegging policies.
The very idea of buffer stocks of finite size necessitates the adaptation of price close to the unregulated market trend. By adding to
demand when price falls and to supply when it rises, on the other
hand, buffer stocks are a suitable tool to even out temporary variations in commodity markets. Other things being equal, the steeper
the demand and supply schedules, the less resources will be required
for the buffer to restore the price to the defended level from a temporary shift in one of the schedules. This is illustrated in Figures
VI.1 A and B, where D_1 and S_1 are the long-run schedules, and
P_2 the equilibrium price. If price decreases to P_1 as a result of a
temporary demand shift to D_2, the buffer stock will have to purchase
quantity Q_3Q_1 to restore price to equilibrium. This quantity is
obviously smaller in Fig. VI.1 B, due to the steepness of the schedules. Similarly, if price falls to P_1, as a result of a temporary
shift of supply to S_2, the buffer will defend the equilibrium price by
buying Q_5Q_3. This is again smaller in Fig. VI.1 B.

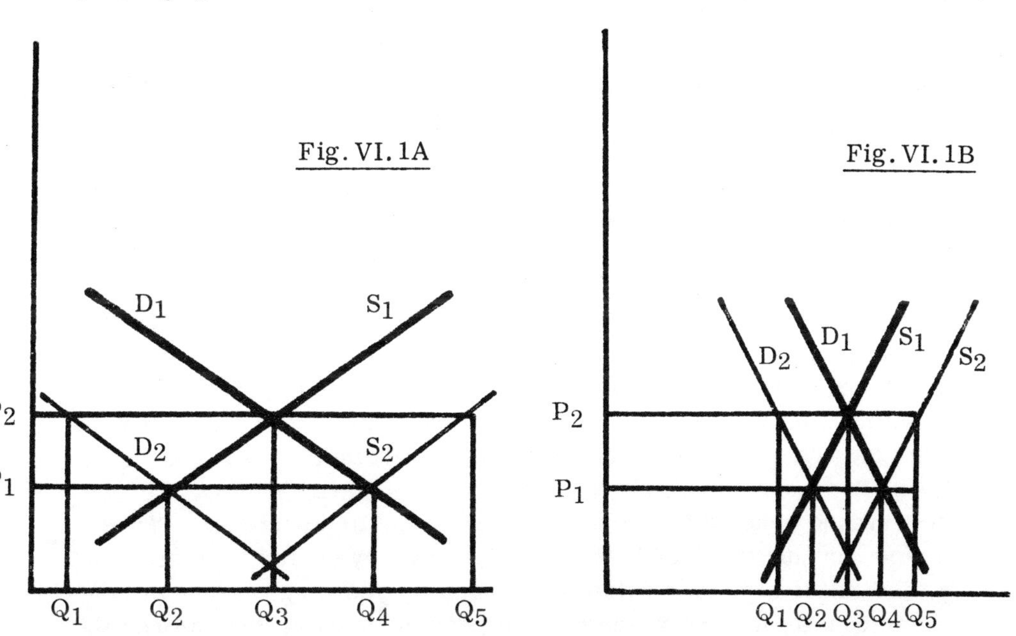

In the actual operations of a buffer, it would hardly be practical to
defend a given price. It is only in theory that the equilibrium price
level is clearly defined. In reality the definiteness will be hazed,
and equilibrium will appear as a price range of smaller or larger

width. Thus the function of the buffer should reasonably be to maintain prices within a specified range. Assuming given price variations, the broader the range, the smaller will be the resources needed by the buffer, to perform its task successfully. With reference to Figure VI.1 again, if the price range to be defended lies between P_1 and P_2, no action will be required by the buffer if demand falls from D_1 to D_2 or if supply rises from S_1 to S_2. The price range will have to be changed in the course of time according to the market trend. If this is not done, the buffer stock will be depleted or else the buffer scheme runs out of money in purchasing at prices above equilibrium. In such situations, a buffer scheme with given resources becomes completely powerless, and can no longer influence the price developments. In principle, the defence of the lower price limit could be continued after the depletion of funds, by mobilizing further money resources from producers or others. If, on the other hand, the buffer stock has been depleted by price pressures on the upper limit, there is nothing more that can be done by the buffer scheme to prevent the price from rising higher.

While depletion of money or stock is a problem in itself, it simultaneously gives an advantage to buffer schemes by acting as a signal that equilibrium prices have probably moved outside the defended range, and that therefore a price adjustment is needed. One could well envisage a rather passive buffer scheme, which would adjust prices downwards or upwards whenever its resources had been emptied. Such a scheme could, nevertheless, be helpful to even out temporary price movements.

In some cases, speculation could muddle this ability of a buffer stock operator to sense the direction of equilibrium price movements. This would happen if speculators were strong in comparison with the resources at the disposal of the scheme. Speculators could then, for instance, empty the buffer by speculative buying, thereby forcing the scheme to increase the price for its purchases. They would run little risk of loss, knowing that they could always resell to the buffer at prices within the original price range. Speculation could equally well be in the other direction, and eventually force the scheme to lower the price range.

Clear-cut grading is a precondition for the use of buffer stocks. The operations will be simplest and cheapest if only one grade exists, like in the case of most metals. Where there are several grades, the efficient operation of a buffer scheme requires sufficient stocks of all the grades, and it will not be possible to utilize scale economies in stock-holding. To ensure stabilization, much larger funds will therefore be required.

Another important limitation with buffer stocks is that they can only be used for storable goods. This excludes such commodities as fresh fruit and meat. A number of commodities like coffee, cocoa, wheat, or copra have a limited durability, and can only be stored in specially constructed warehouses. Buffer stocks of such commodities are possible, but they have to be turned over regularly, and the storage charges will be high. It follows therefore that buffer stock schemes are best suited to minerals, and possible but less efficient for easily storable and durable agricultural commodities.

An international buffer stock is costly to operate. Transport and storage, interest on capital invested, and sometimes depreciation of value constitute the main cost items in operating a buffer scheme. They could hardly be less than 10% of the average stock value per year. For commodities which require special storage arrangements, costs will probably be still higher. In addition to the problem of cost there is the difficulty of getting the credit required to run a buffer scheme. The size of the stock will have to be determined in relation to total world turnover, and the short-term volatility of the market. Even a relatively limited buffer stock will require substantial funds. To build up a rubber buffer, amounting to 200,000 tons - which corresponds to some 5% of the yearly world turnover - would have required $100 million at 1964 prices. An average buffer of this size would consequently cost at least $10 million per year to run. This expenditure could by no means guarantee price stability, if yearly variations in supply or demand exceeded 5%.

The overall cost of international buffer stocks to producers, traders and users could be lower, if the expected price stability could convince them to cut down their own stocks. It is not possible to predict with certainty what will happen to private stock-holding, when a buffer stock is established. Possibly the short-run effect on private stocks would be insignificant. In the long run, if the international buffer proves successful in maintaining prices at predictable levels, a sizeable reduction of other stocks could be brought about. Even if this happened, it still seems improbable that the producer and user gains could be extracted to finance the international buffer.

In principle, the operation of a buffer stock, with a policy to buy cheap and sell dear, should result in a surplus, to cover at least part of the operating costs. In reality the market conditions are so complicated that even the most experienced buffer manager can easily miss profitable opportunities. A stock of goods always runs the risk of becoming unsaleable, by change of fashion or technique. A stock of primary commodities is perhaps not so sensitive to fashion changes. On the other hand, new developments can easily transfer demand between grades, and a stock manager may find himself with unsold supplies of a variety which can only be realized at a loss. A persistently downward-directed price trend, necessitating consecutively lower price ranges, will also result in a capital loss for the scheme in terms of other goods.

The substantial amounts of credit needed, the high operating costs and the risks of capital losses together with the uncertainty of the gains to be derived from stabilization of prices are the main explanatory factors for the limited use of international buffer stocks. U-countries maintain that they cannot afford the costs. I-countries are also unwilling to extend the use of buffer stocks because of the amounts involved.

For a number of years there has been a long-drawn-out discussion about the establishment of an international buffer stock for cocoa. The main factor preventing an agreement from being signed has been disagreement about the distribution of costs. In the summer of 1967, a proposal was hammered out jointly by the USA and Ghana, the largest importer and exporter, regarding the rules according to which an agreement should be operated. It is taken up here because of its novel features with regard to buffer stock operations, and in particular to the distribution of the cost burden. Like in the case of tin, this agreement would combine export quotas with a buffer stock. The finance for the buffer would be provided by producers' contributions. A price range would be established, and quotas enforced, when prices fell below the minimum. Producers would be able to sell to the buffer any output above their quotas, but at a price of only 50% of the minimum of the range. If at a later date the buffer succeeded to sell this cocoa at the maximum of the range, producers who had supplied to the buffer would receive a bonus. In this way the cost of operation and the risk of capital loss for the scheme are limited. A further provision maximizes the buffer stock at 250,000 tons. Buffer purchases above that would only be made at prices so low that the cocoa could be profitably used in a non-traditional way, namely in the production of margarine.[1] Despite

the US-Ghana agreement, and the innovations proposed to reduce
the costs of running the scheme, there have not been any reports of
the start of its operation. Could it be that the producing side, which
would carry the main burden, and obtain a fairly hollow price
stabilization in return, has found the burden too heavy in comparison
with the possible advantages?

VI.2   Effects on revenue from international buffer stock schemes

An international buffer scheme can achieve its target - maintenance
of prices within a predetermined range - if adequate resources are
at its disposal. But if it succeeds in this primary objective, what
will be the effects on the export revenue stabilization and on the total
export proceeds over a full cycle, in comparison with the unregulated market, where prices are allowed to vary freely? In the
following we will be making the simplifying assumption that, in the
absence of buffers, price will move at regular time intervals
between two levels, and that the establishment of a buffer stock will
stabilize it exactly in the middle between the two extremes. Linear
functions will be assumed throughout. For the answer to the question
just posed, viz. effects on revenue stability, reference is made to
section 3 in chapter I, where it is seen that price stabilization can
lead to both higher stability and to instability, depending on whether
demand or supply is shifting, and on the price elasticities of the
demand and supply schedules.

Total revenue can also be affected both ways by the introduction of
buffer stocks. The results will differ depending on the underlying
conditions, and several different cases must be considered.

Variable supply

The first case to be taken up is one where demand remains
unchanged, while supply varies in a regular cycle but is fixed during
each market period, independently of the then prevailing prices.
The coffee market, with short-run supply depending on the harvest
outcome, can be said to resemble this situation to some extent.
Total revenue from exports will ordinarily be increased in this case,
when price movements are evened out. Figure VI.2 A illustrates
this. If supply varies between Q_1 and Q_3, total revenue over the
two periods will be $P_3Q_1 + P_1Q_3$. With a buffer stabilizing prices
at P_2, the two-period revenue will be $P_2Q_1 + P_2Q_3 = 2P_2Q_2$,

88

(note that $Q_1Q_2 = Q_2Q_3$), which is larger than when prices vary.
Figure VI. 2 B provides a generalization of this case. With stabilization, the two-period revenue will be $2TR_2$; without stabilization,
it will only amount to $2TR_1$. The gain from stabilizing a given
relative price swing will increase with the price elasticity of demand.
There will be a gain as long as the total revenue schedule is concave
from below, e.g. as long as the marginal revenue schedule is decreasing. If the average and marginal revenues are constant, and
the total revenue schedule is consequently a straight line, total
revenue will be unaffected by price stabilization. Only in the unusual
case where the total revenue schedule is convex from below, and
the marginal revenue is consequently increasing over the relevant
range, would price stabilization result in a loss of revenue to the
exporting side over the two periods.

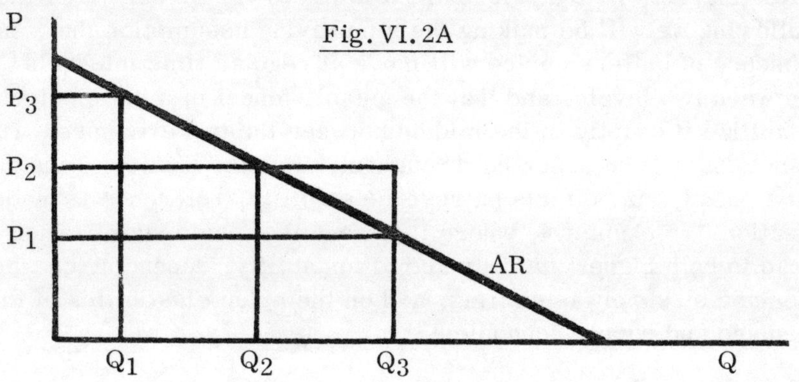

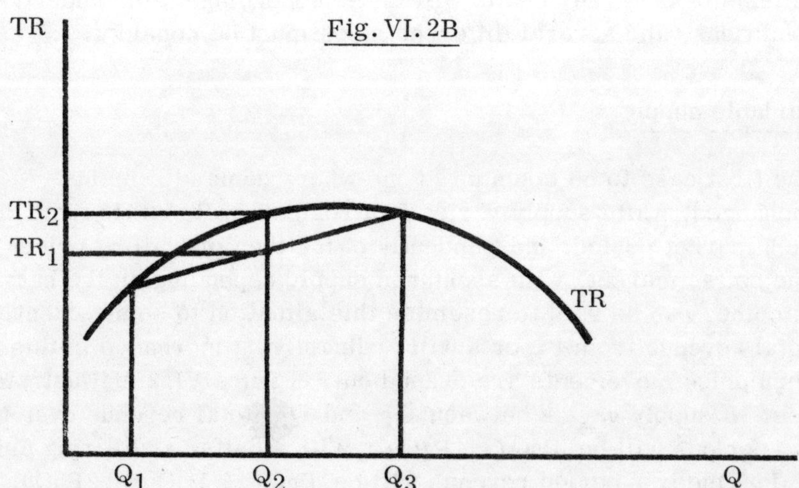

How significant could the gains in revenue be? Rough calculations, assuming linear demand functions, and 25% price swings to either side of the average, produce a revenue gain of less than 4%, when price elasticity of demand is 0.5. The gain increases to more than 14% of revenue, when the demand elasticity is 1.5 (see Figure VI.3 A and VI.3 B). How does this compare with the buffer stock costs? From Figure VI.3 A we get a maximum necessary stock-holding of Q_3Q_2/OQ_2, or approximately 11% of turnover, when elasticity is 0.5. Calculating an overall cost of buffer operations at 15% on this maximum stock, we get total buffer costs amounting to less than 2% of turnover, as compared with the 4% gain from stabilization. A buffer therefore appears to result in a net gain. Similarly, in Figure VI.3 B, with elasticity at 1.5, maximum stock-holding would be Q_3Q_2/OQ_2, or almost 50% of turnover. With the same cost assumption of 15%, the buffer operation would cost less than 8% of turnover, and would result in a net gain to the producing side. It should not be forgotten that the producer gain, considered here, will be the result of higher outlay in the purchase of the commodity by the importing side.

Before drawing any hasty conclusions, we must remind ourselves of the many simplifying assumptions underlying the above results. We assume a known, linear and stable demand function. We assume completely regular price movements, both with regard to time and magnitude. This relieves us of the necessity of additional precautionary stock-holding. On these assumptions a buffer stock seems to be profitable for the producing countries. In the real world, however, such purified conditions are not likely to be found.

Variable demand

The second case is one of a stable supply schedule, and a regularly occurring parallel shift in demand. The market for copper or tin could be said to resemble this situation. So long as production is undisturbed by strikes and suchlike, supply will be stable. Demand, on the other hand, will have a tendency to fluctuate with the business cycles in i-countries. Total revenue from exports will ordinarily be decreased in this case by price stabilization through a buffer stock. The simplest situation is depicted in Figure VI.4. The total revenue over the full cycle with variable prices will be $P_1Q_1 + P_3Q_3$, which is higher than $2P_2Q_2$, the revenue over the same period with price variations evened out.

G

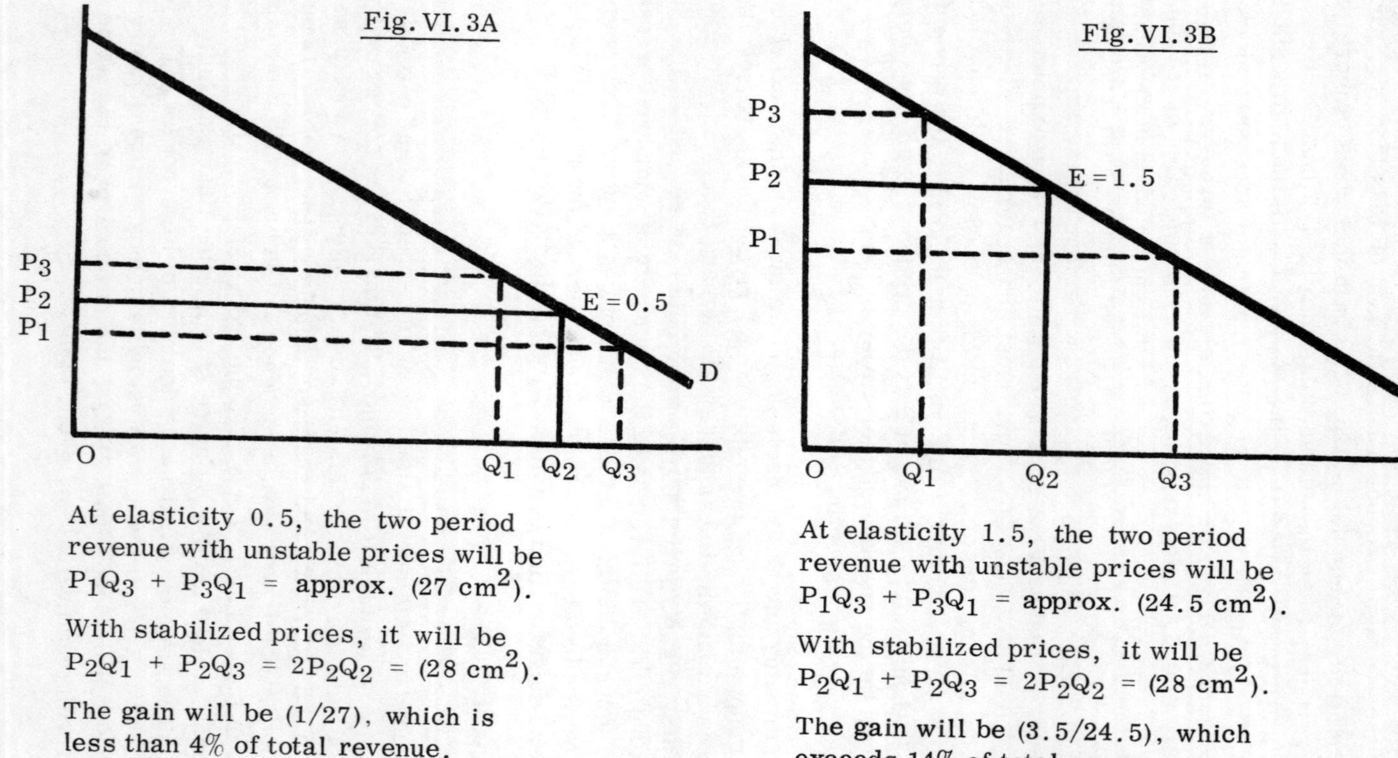

At elasticity 0.5, the two period revenue with unstable prices will be $P_1Q_3 + P_3Q_1$ = approx. (27 cm^2).

With stabilized prices, it will be $P_2Q_1 + P_2Q_3 = 2P_2Q_2$ = (28 cm^2).

The gain will be (1/27), which is less than 4% of total revenue.

At elasticity 1.5, the two period revenue with unstable prices will be $P_1Q_3 + P_3Q_1$ = approx. (24.5 cm^2).

With stabilized prices, it will be $P_2Q_1 + P_2Q_3 = 2P_2Q_2$ = (28 cm^2).

The gain will be (3.5/24.5), which exceeds 14% of total revenue.

It seems that this market situation has received more attention in
literature than the one with varying supply schedules considered
before. Snape and Yamey carry out quite a number of exercises
with the basic assumptions given above.[2]   What they analyze is,
among other things, the effect on producer income from the establishment of national buffer funds. Their conclusions are fully
applicable to the problem considered here. They vary the assumptions of Figure VI.4 by considering different elasticities for the
supply and demand schedules, and also by assuming a home demand.
Without going into the analytical details, their conclusions are

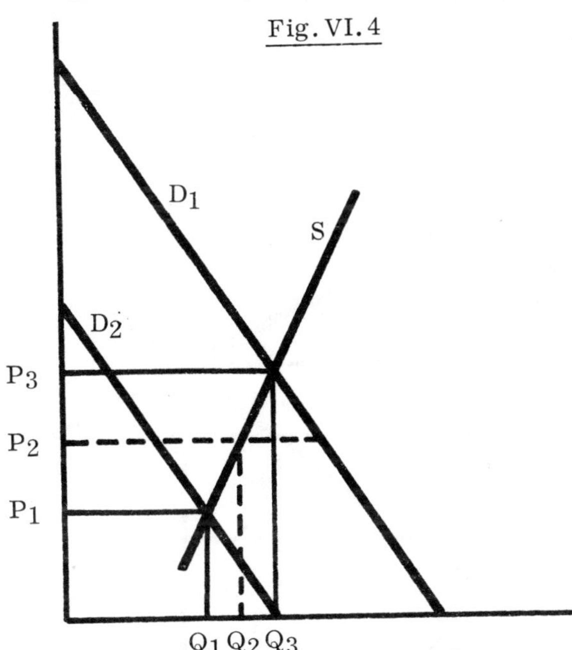

Fig. VI. 4

reproduced in Table VI.1. The results appear to confirm the
conclusion drawn from Fig.VI.4, which in fact corresponds to case
5 A in the table. In most ordinary market situations, a price-
stabilizing buffer will lead to smaller export revenue. Only in
some unusual cases, with an unlikely reaction in home demand
(4 B and 8a.B) or where the supply elasticity is negative, would a
buffer unequivocally result in a gain to the producing side.

H. G. Grubel has studied the effects of non-parallel shifts in the
demand schedule.[3] He first concludes, along the lines of Fig. VI. 4,

that with insignificant home demand, positive supply elasticity and parallel shifts of demand, a buffer stock will cause a loss of revenue to producers. If, however, the higher demand schedule is flatter than the lower one, the loss to producers from a buffer stock will diminish, and will eventually be converted into a gain. Figure VI.5 illustrates this. The two-period unregulated revenue will be P_1Q_1 + P_3Q_3. With a buffer stock, price has to be set at P_2, because at this level the excess quantity supplied during the demand slack equals the excess quantity demanded during boom. The producers' two-period revenue with a buffer will be $2P_2Q_2$, which turns out to be higher than when price is allowed to vary. The producer gain of revenue will diminish with increasing steepness of D_2 in relation to D_1.

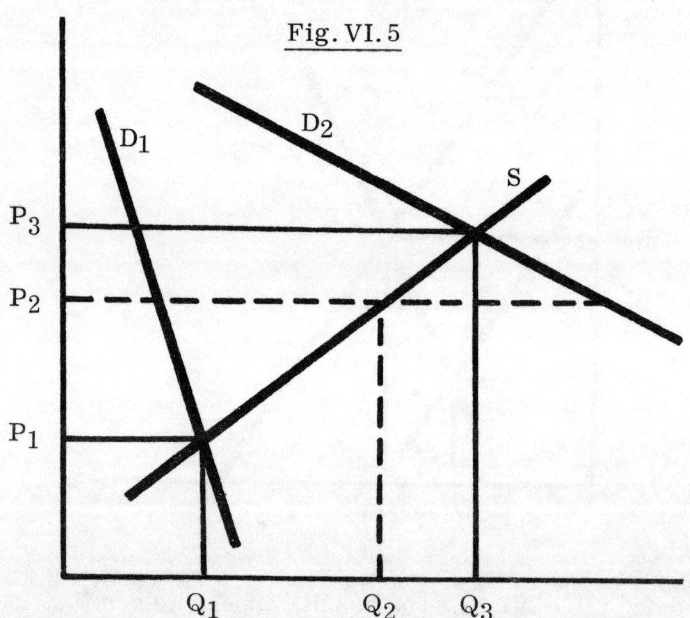

Grubel then discusses the demand change likely to occur during a boom. On theoretical grounds he concludes that the boom demand schedule will probably be steeper because, during the boom, substitution is less likely to occur. This confirms our earlier contention that buffer stocks would ordinarily not be profitable to the producer side, when price variations are caused by shifts in the demand schedule.

Again, we should not forget the simplifying assumptions used in this case, e.g. linear functions, complete cyclical regularity, etc., which are necessary to simplify the analysis, but which simultaneously remove it from real world conditions.

<u>Lagged supply</u>

The situation becomes much more complex if we assume lagged supply patterns, and then try to consider the effects of buffers on the revenue of the producing side. A multiplicity of results can be obtained, where either the exporting or the importing side could gain from the establishment of buffer stocks. As an illustration, a case of a one-period lag in the supply reaction, and the demand schedule steeper than supply, is depicted in Figure VI.6. The equilibrating intersection between demand and supply is unstable, and once it has been disturbed by an exogenous shock, a diverging cobweb pattern will ensue. Some horticultural markets have tended to experience developments like the ones referred to here.

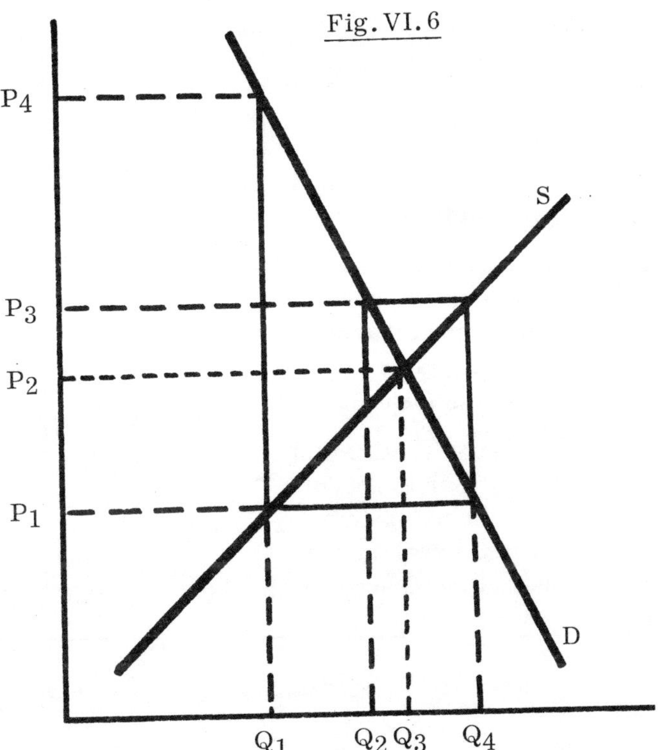

Table VI.1   <u>Changes in producer receipts as a result of the operation of a price evening buffer scheme</u>

Price elasticity of supply			A Positive	B Zero	C Negative
Export demand infinitely elastic		Home demand schedule:			
		1. No home demand	S	U	G
		2. The same in each year	S	U	G
		3. Shifts in same direction as export demand schedule	S	S	G/S
		4. Shifts in opposite direction to export demand schedule	G/S	G	G/S
Export demand not infinitely elastic		5. No home demand	S	U	G
		6. The same in each year	S	U	G/S
		7. Shifts in same direction as export demand schedule	S	S	G/S
		8a. Shifts in opposite direction to export demand schedule – with buffer fund scheme, export price higher in year when export demand higher	G/S	G	G/S
		8b. Shifts in opposite direction to export demand schedule – with buffer fund scheme, export price lower in year when export demand higher	S	S	G/S

G = greater, U = unaffected, S = smaller, G/S = greater or smaller or unaffected.

Source: Snape & Yamey, 'A Diagrammatic Analysis of some effects of Buffer Fund Stabilization', <u>Oxford Economic Papers</u>, New Series, Vol.15, July 1963, p.102.

The stable revenue per period will be P_2Q_3. The exogenous disturbance in the form of supply Q_2, short of Q_3, has to be countered by buffer sales if equilibrium is to be maintained. Otherwise supply and demand will spiral away from equilibrium, as illustrated in the figure. Total export revenue for the first three periods will be as follows. Numbers denote cm.^{2} in Figure VI.6.

Period	With buffer		cumulative	Without buffer		cumulative
1	P_2Q_3	25	25	P_3Q_2	27	27
2	P_2Q_3	25	50	P_1Q_4	18	45
3	P_2Q_3	25	75	P_4Q_1	27	72

Under the conditions assumed in this situation, producers' revenue will be larger over several periods with a buffer scheme.

Further considerations on revenue

Real market conditions will probably carry features of all three situations, and in addition will be influenced by further factors not considered here. In view of this, it is hardly possible to reach a definite and general conclusion as to whether buffer stock schemes increase the export revenue of producing countries. One could perhaps dare a cautious conclusion that revenue gains are likely to accrue to producers when buffers even out price variations mainly due to shifts in supply, and that revenue losses are probable if prices vary due mainly to variable demand.

Proceeding one further cautious step in this argument, one might say that instability from varying supply can be said to be caused by the exporting side, while instability from shifting demand is the result of conditions and policies in importing countries. If the benefits from price stability are equally desirable to both the importing and the exporting side, then it might be reasonable that the side which causes price instability should also pay for stabilization measures. According to this argument, therefore, exporters ought to pay the buffer scheme costs when instability is caused by supply changes, while importers take over when unstable prices result from demand variations.

The argument could be used to frame general principles, but would not be of great help in devising a detailed policy. First of all, our knowledge of demand and supply conditions, and the shifts which occur, is very incomplete. Secondly, "ability to pay" considerations must be kept in view, when deciding on commodity stabilization measures. Furthermore, an agreement on the division of costs will be the result of bargaining, where political evaluations rather than economic gains or arguments of justice play the most important role.

VI.3 An approximation of resource requirements in the Tin Agreement

We recall from our discussion of the tin agreement in chapter III that the market is to be regulated through a combination of export restrictions and a buffer stock. We also recall that since around 1960, the resources of the buffer amount to £20 million in direct contributions, and an additional £10 million in credit-drawing facility – a total of £30 million. As appears from Chart III.2, the agreement was completely unsuccessful during 1964, 1965 and part of 1966 in keeping the price level between the predetermined ranges. Apparently the main reason for this was lack of tin metal stocks in the buffer. As mentioned earlier, it is easier for a buffer stock to defend the minimum price because, if price tends to fall below this level, additional cash resources could always be mobilized to buy more of the commodity into the buffer. The maximum of the range can be defended only so long as the commodity is available with the scheme. In the period reviewed here, the tin agreement, completely lacking in resources of tin, was defenceless against the upward price pressures. In 1962, the buffer succeeded – obtaining an insignificant amount of 3,200 tons of tin, which was then sold at the beginning of 1963. In the years which will be considered here, the tin buffer had no metal stocks at all. Retrospectively it is easy to point out that the decision on price ranges was not particularly successful in hitting the equilibrium level. Be that as it may, our task will now be to try to estimate the amount of tin in the buffer required to keep the price within the range during the period November 1963 to May 1966, when the price was above the maximum of the range established by the Tin Agreement.

Luckily, from the point of view of our investigation, the export restriction measures in the tin agreement are inoperative when price tends to rise above the agreed limits, and we can study the possible effects of a buffer stock in isolation. The important variables to be considered should be market supply, demand and price.

All figures have been collected from the International Tin Council
Monthly Statistical Bulletin. The price series used are those for
cash transactions at the London Metal Exchange. In view of the
absence of trade restrictions in major consuming countries, and
close contacts between the important tin markets, the London prices
give a fairly reliable picture of the tin price movements.

The demand and supply magnitudes are much more difficult to
determine. The ITC statistics estimate what they call consumption
and production. Consumption probably includes most additions to
users' stocks, as these stocks are not externally visible. [4] Lacking
better figures, we take the ITC consumption figure at its face value,
and assume it to be equal to demand. Similarly we take supply as
equal to production, with one qualification. Since the end of 1962,
considerable amounts of tin have been released for sale by the US
strategic stock. We add those sales to the ITC production estimate,
to arrive at our supply figure.

These demand and supply quantities, when compared, give a somewhat unexpected result. Since 1965, according to the figures,
quantity consumed in per cent of quantity supplied has amounted to:

1956	1957	1958	1959	1960	1961	1962	1963
90	90	112	130	111	115	111	107

Thus, from 1958, consumption seems to have been persistently
higher than supply. Yet, known stocks, excluding the ITA buffer and
the US strategic stockpile, have not undergone any significant change
between 1958 and 1963 (see section on tin agreement in chapter III.
US strategic stock additions are not known.) From the apparent
excess demand situation since 1958, one would expect constant
upward pressures on prices. A glance at Chart II.2 indicates that
prices remained relatively stable. The strong upward push started
only in 1963, when the excess demand had diminished. To get a
more detailed picture of the period to be studied, we present Chart
VI.1, which consists of two parts. The upper part is a reproduction
of the relevant portion of Chart III.2 showing the monthly price
movements in relation to the ranges defended by the buffer. The
lower part shows monthly production of tin, to which have been
added the US strategic stock releases. This estimated supply is
then compared with the monthly consumption or demand figures over
the same period. A visual analysis of the years 1964-66 conveys
the same lack of correlation between excess demand and price as

for the longer period discussed above. In 1964, supply seems to have been larger than demand, while prices rose to extreme levels. In 1966, when supply and demand appear to be more or less equal, prices have been falling consistently.

Two explanations could be provided to account for the lack of correlation between the variation of excess demand and the price movements. The first is that the development of prices has been caused by other factors than current supply and demand conditions. Expectations about future production expansion or contraction could for instance have influenced the price formation. The second explanation could be that the ITC production or consumption figures have been inaccurately estimated.

Let us select supply as our basic variable, and this for two reasons: first because, production being more concentrated than use, the supply figure is likely to be the more reliable of the two; and secondly because, during the period to be studied, price is continuously above the desired level, and buffer action will therefore be on the supply side only. Let us further assume that prices in the tin market are formed in accordance with the simple mechanism outlined in section I.4, i.e. they fall with increased supply and rise when supply is curtailed. To estimate how a buffer stock addition to supply will affect price, we must also make some assumptions about the demand elasticity for tin. Knowing that tin, like lead and zinc, lacks close substitutes, and concluding therefrom that the demand elasticities of the three commodities will not be very dissimilar, [5] we will base our calculations on a short-term demand elasticity for tin at 0.5. A further simplifying assumption to facilitate our calculations will be that this demand elasticity remains invariant over the price and quantity changes considered here.

Table VI.2 summarizes our calculations. If the actual price exceeds by 1% the maximum price level of the ITA, an increase by 0.5% of the actual supply should, according to the above assumption, decrease price by 1% and bring it within the buffer range. The number of tons to be supplied by the buffer each month is thus easily calculated. Over the whole 31-month period of actual excess prices, the necessary buffer sales would have amounted to some 31,000 tons. Assuming an earlier purchase price for the buffer at £1,000 per ton, the £30 million at the disposal of the tin buffer manager would seem more or less sufficient to counter this particular short-term (31-month) price swing, provided that the total buffer resources had been in the form of tin in November 1963.

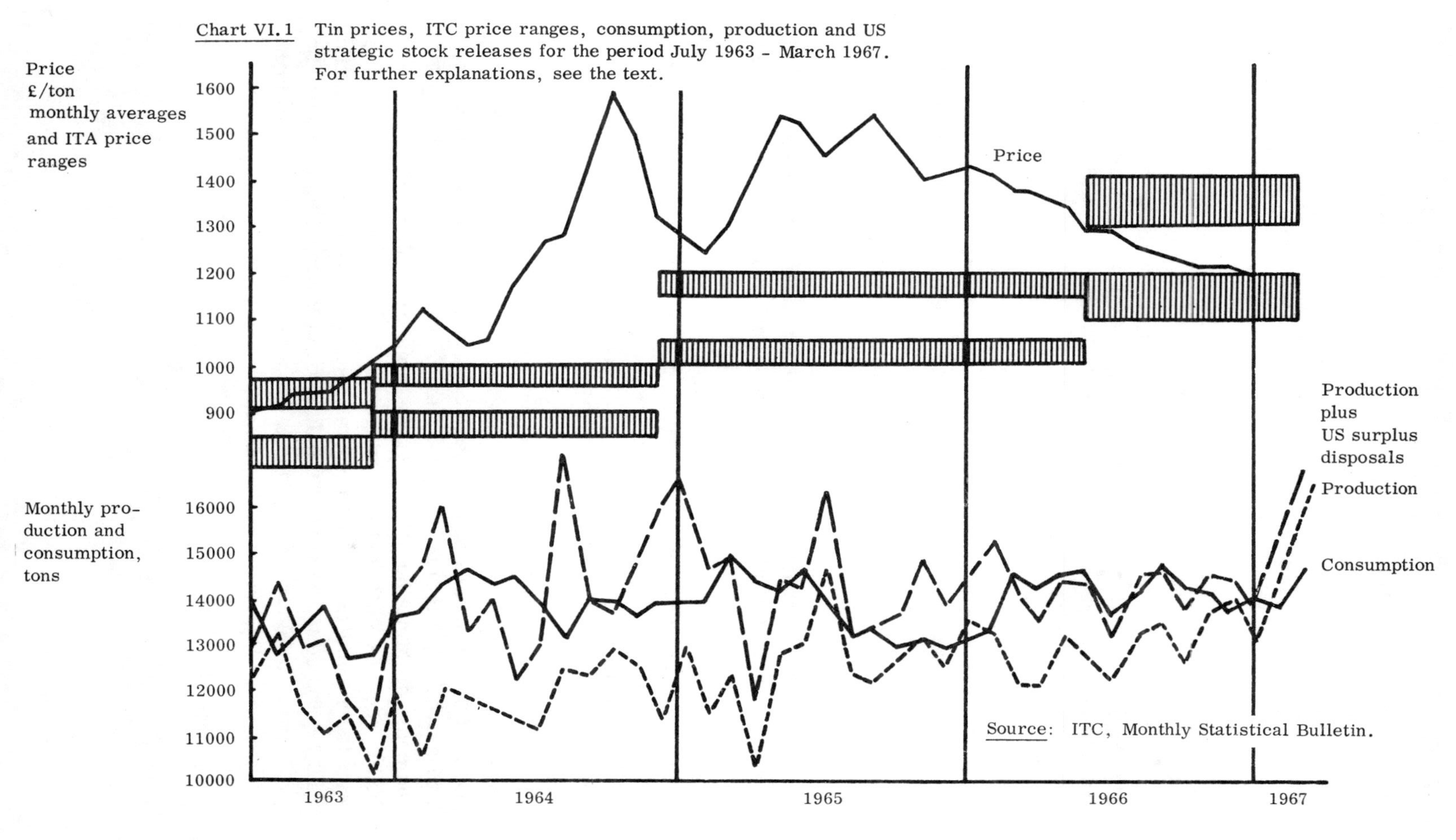

Chart VI.1   Tin prices, ITC price ranges, consumption, production and US strategic stock releases for the period July 1963 – March 1967. For further explanations, see the text.
Price
£/ton
monthly averages
and ITA price
ranges
1600
1500
1400
1300
1200
1100
1000
900
Price
Production
plus
US surplus
disposals
Production
Monthly pro-
duction and
consumption,
tons
16000
15000
14000
13000
12000
11000
10000
Consumption
Source: ITC, Monthly Statistical Bulletin.
1963
1964
1965
1966
1967

Several problems - which will not be further pursued - need to be mentioned here. The first considers the effects which the earlier buffer purchases of 31,000 tons would have had on price. With all probability, such large purchases, even if spread over several years, would have pushed the price above the range in the years 1956-63.

The second fairly self-evident point is that if the buffer had placed all its resources in tin by November 1963, it would have been completely defenceless against a different market development from what in fact occurred. Having no cash, the buffer could not have prevented the prices from falling.

Thirdly, we should note from Chart VI.1 that the US stock sales were highest during 1964, the year which experienced the sharpest price increases. In that year almost 29,000 tons were supplied from the US stock. In the absence of these sales, the buffer would have required this additional amount at its disposal for operations in 1964 only.

Fourthly, it is retrospectively easy to conclude that the buffer resource requirements would have been much smaller if the price ranges had been established at higher levels during 1964 and 1965. At that time, however, the ranges must have appeared as reasonable approximations of the then prevailing equilibrium.

In view of the above considerations it seems reasonable that the tin buffer stock would need to increase its present resources more than twice over if it is to have a fair chance of being successful in neutralizing the many market disturbances, and so maintain prices within ranges as narrow as the ones established by the ITC up to now. A strengthening of the scheme on this scale would indeed be expensive. Up till now, the producers have covered practically all the costs of the tin buffer stock. It is questionable whether the buffer renders sufficient advantages to the producing side, to warrant the expanded costs. This question should be posed in particular with reference to the cost of the defence of the maximum price. Do producers, in other words, find it reasonable to incur expenditure on this scale to prevent prices from rising?

Table VI.2   An estimate of tin supply increases needed to maintain tin prices within the ITC range.

For explanations, see the text.

A Month	B Supply: Production plus US surplus disposal (tons)	C Actual price (£/ton cash LME)	D Maximum price level of upper range of the ITA (£/ton)	E Excess of actual price over maximum price level of upper range in % of actual price $\frac{C-D}{C}$	F Necessary increase in supply in % of total supply $\frac{E}{2}$	G Necessary increase in supply in tons $F \cdot B$
1963 Nov	11,800	975	960	1.5	0.75	90
Dec	11,100	1,010	1,000	1.0	0.5	50
1964 Jan	13,900	1,041	1,000	3.9	2.0	280
Feb	14,600	1,109	1,000	9.8	4.9	720
Mar	15,900	1,073	1,000	7.2	3.6	570
Apr	13,200	1,043	1,000	4.1	2.1	270
May	13,800	1,054	1,000	5.1	2.6	350
Jun	12,200	1,183	1,000	15.5	7.8	940
Jul	12,800	1,251	1,000	20.1	10.0	1,280
Aug	17,100	1,271	1,000	21.3	10.6	1,820
Sep	13,900	1,425	1,000	29.8	14.9	2,070
Oct	13,600	1,584	1,000	36.8	18.4	2,510
Nov	14,500	1,488	1,000	32.8	16.4	2,380
Dec	15,800	1,317	1,200	8.9	4.4	710
1965 Jan	16,700	1,254	1,200	4.3	2.2	360
Feb	14,500	1,230	1,200	2.4	1.2	180
Mar	14,900	1,300	1,200	7.7	3.9	570
Apr	11,700	1,430	1,200	15.8	7.9	920
May	14,300	1,530	1,200	21.6	10.8	1,540
Jun	14,200	1,500	1,200	20.0	10.0	1,420
Jul	16,300	1,440	1,200	16.7	8.3	1,360
Aug	13,100	1,484	1,200	19.2	9.6	1,250
Sep	13,300	1,527	1,200	21.4	10.7	1,420
Oct	13,700	1,455	1,200	17.5	8.8	1,200
Nov	14,800	1,386	1,200	13.4	6.7	1,000
Dec	13,700	1,405	1,200	14.6	7.3	1,000
1966 Jan	14,400	1,425	1,200	15.8	7.9	1,140
Feb	15,200	1,407	1,200	14.6	7.3	1,110
Mar	14,000	1,370	1,200	12.4	6.2	870
Apr	13,400	1,365	1,200	12.0	6.0	800
May	14,400	1,340	1,200	10.4	5.2	750
					Total	30,930

VI.4 <u>A commodity buffer stock as reserve currency</u>

In the contemporary discussion about international liquidity problems, a number of proposals emphasize that new additions to liquidity should be used in the first instance to help u-countries in their development planning and foreign exchange difficulties. A few of them propose a direct link between the new liquidity and the commodity markets. It has for instance been suggested in FAO circles that additions to world liquidity should primarily be used to finance new international commodity agreements, such as for example maintenance of buffer stocks in the case of cocoa. Another line of thought has been that the new liquidity could be used for compensatory payments to countries producing commodities which experience a price decline, much in the same way as deficiency payments are made to support domestic farm incomes in a number of i-countries. [6]

Perhaps the most thought-provoking of the suggestions in this line is the Hart-Kaldor-Tinbergen "Case for an International Reserve Currency", fully presented at the UNCTAD Conference in 1964. [7] Through their proposal, the authors wish to solve three problems simultaneously, namely that of international liquidity, that of instability of commodity markets, and finally also that of exchange scarcity and the slow pace of development in u-countries.

To ease the international liquidity scarcity, the authors suggest that gold, dollars, pounds and drawing rights on the IMF could be supplemented by a reserve consisting of primary commodity stocks, owned and operated by IMF. IMF would create a new currency, called Bancor, convertible either into gold or into the commodity stocks held by it. Bancor would be a true reserve currency, used exclusively by central banks. Originally IMF might issue the equivalent of US $ 30 billion of Bancor, out of which $ 5 billion should be exchanged for gold, another $ 5 billion for loan obligations of member countries, while $ 20 billion would be used to acquire stocks of commodities according to specified procedures. Member governments would agree to accept certain amounts of Bancor in exchange for gold and commodities.

The number of commodities to be included in the IMF stock should be as large as possible. For inclusion in the IMF bundle the commodities must be standardized and durable. The relative proportions of the different commodities to be purchased into the

IMF stock would be fixed beforehand. IMF would acquire the commodities, either from member governments or in the open market, at or below a specified price, and sell them when their price rose above a declared limit. Thus the scheme would operate like a huge multi-commodity buffer stock. Storage and interest costs for operating the scheme would be debited to member governments.

According to the authors, this arrangement would automatically lead to a stabilization of average commodity prices. In addition, and this seems to be the most important theme in the argument, an increased supply of commodities would automatically lead to larger issues of Bancor, resulting in higher liquidity in commodity-producing countries, and a consequently higher demand from these for manufactured goods from i-countries, this in turn adding to the i-countries' demand for primary commodities. A reversed self-balancing process would follow if primary commodity prices started to rise. Broadly speaking, there would be a correlation between increases in the supply of commodities, international liquidity and demand for manufactured goods. On the basis of larger supplies of primary commodities an expansion would have to take place in manufacturing industries to meet the additional demand for manufactured goods. The authors suggest that today's i-countries, in view of scarce labor resources and an unwillingness to acquire too large trade surpluses, might be unable to provide for all this expansion. The result would be a process of industrialization of u-countries, and an eventual evening out of the economic differences between u- and i-countries.

The Hart-Kaldor-Tinbergen proposal, like so many other commodity arrangement schemes, lacks a proper statement of its primary objective. In trying to pursue no less than three somewhat diffusely defined aims, it becomes intricate and difficult to analyze.

An IMF-buffer, as envisaged here, would be very costly to maintain and operate. It is likely that world total stocks of the IMF-bundle commodities would increase through the buffer creation. With the uncertainty of the scheme's future, commercial and strategic stocks at national and sub-national levels would probably not be diminished by an amount corresponding to the buffer value.

The scheme would quite probably lead to an average stabilization of commodity prices. It may be doubted, however, if the prices of individual commodities would also be stabilized. The resource

transfers which the scheme is to accomplish are neither equitable
(for a discussion of equitability through commodity arrangements,
see section VII.4) nor simple to achieve politically.

The contribution of the scheme towards the solution of the world's
liquidity problems is not as clear-cut as the authors desire to make
it appear. First of all there is no direct correlation between total
world trade and trade in commodities. Trade in manufactures has
in fact been increasing at a faster rate than commodity trade. To
give a proper support to commodity price stability, the reserve
creating buffer stock should be increased parallel with the growth of
commodity trade. World liquidity, on the other hand, needs additions proportional to total world trade. Thus there appears a lack
of consistency between two of the aims pursued.

Neither is there any clear-cut relationship between the volume of
industrial production and commodity consumption. Industrial innovations often result in savings in the use of raw materials in
manufacturing. As a result, the economic development relation-
ships which the authors emphasize in their scheme become
somewhat less certain.

Many of the problems inherent in buffer stock operations, discussed
earlier in this chapter, would affect this proposal in equal measure.
Furthermore, a scheme with so many novel features would require
some very bold political decision-making. In view of doubts of its
success and current political differences regarding the solution of
the world liquidity problems, the scheme is hardly likely to be
brought into operation.

Notes and references to Chapter VI

1)   Economist, Oct.14, 1967, p.212.

2)   Snape and Yamey, 'A Diagrammatic Analysis of some effects
      of Buffer Fund Stabilization', Oxford Economic Papers, New
      Series, Vol.15, July 1963.

3)   H.G.Grubel, 'Foreign Exchange Earnings and Price
      Stabilization Schemes', American Economic Review, June 1964.

4)   J.W.F.Rowe, <u>Primary Commodities in International Trade</u>, Cambridge 1965, p.41.

5)   Estimates of the short-run demand elasticity of lead and zinc give values under or about 0.5. See UNCTAD Comm. problems and policies, TD/8/Suppl.1, 14 Nov., 1967, stencil p.60.

6)   FAO Monthly Bulletin, March 1966, p.1-9.

7)   UNCTAD I, New York 1964, Proceedings, Vol.III, p.522-538.

H

VII ARE COMPENSATORY FINANCE SCHEMES SUPERIOR TO COMMODITY AGREEMENTS?

VII.1 <u>Background to the growing discussion</u>

Since the middle of the 1950's there has been a lively discussion,
particularly in UN circles, about alternative strategies for tackling
the commodity instability problems of u-countries. More and more
attention has been directed to compensatory finance as an alternative and more efficient measure to bring about the objectives
desired.

A substantial step forward in the theoretical discussion was taken
by Nurkse and others in two symposia arranged by <u>Kyklos</u> in 1958
and 1959. [1]) In his article[2]), Nurkse criticizes buffer stock
schemes as wasteful and inefficient, and instead proposes national
fiscal measures to counter export revenue instability. He has a
strong belief in the ability of primary-commodity-exporting u-
countries to reallocate factors of production between the export and
domestic sectors in response to fluctuating export prices. From
this he concludes that a general income and profit tax during an
export boom and a corresponding subsidy during export slump,
falling equally on the domestic and export sectors, would be a
purposeful stabilization policy. He rejects a policy stabilizing export
revenue through consecutive export taxes and subsidies, because
such a policy would not create the slack in export industries which
is needed to induce factors to move out of the export sector. A
general anticyclical taxation program as mentioned above, on the
other hand, could maintain stability within the economy as a whole,
while simultaneously allowing the instability in the export sector to
work with full force, and thereby induce factor reallocation between
the export and home sectors.

Nurkse's policy recipe follows the neoclassical tradition in assuming perfection in many features of the economy. As a practical
program for u-countries it **is perhaps** less useful in view of the

experienced immobility of factors of production, the absence of an efficiently functioning price system, and a considerable hidden or open unemployment (see also section I.3). A further problem of a more practical relevance is the difficulty of carrying through income- or profit-taxation programs in u-countries, and in particular to make them as flexbible as would be required to counter the shifting export cycles.

Nurkse's central points, namely that the export sector fluctuations should not be levelled out, but that the economy as a whole benefits from stabilization measures to counter the instability generated by foreign trade, reappear in various forms in the compensatory finance proposals.

The emergence of the more practical discussion on compensatory finance schemes has at least three major causes. The first is the difficulty experienced in establishing and running commodity agreements. In spite of prolonged efforts, only four truly international commodity agreements are functioning at the present time. Not until recently has it been possible to revive the long-dormant sugar agreement. Repetitious and dragged-out negotiations on a cocoa agreement have not so far led to any results of substance. There seems to be a considerable difficulty in expanding the commodity agreement coverage very much wider than it has reached at present. This unwillingness may in part be explained by the difficulties experienced in running a commodity agreement, once it has been established. The practical experience of post-war years hardly seems encouraging and there are many theoretical objections as well to the efficiency of the tools used in achieving stability or an increase in long-run proceeds. These have been spelled out in earlier chapters.

The second cause of the discussion is that compensatory finance measures seem to offer an opportunity to decrease instability of price or revenue without direct and perhaps harmful intervention in the commodity markets. It is said that the commodity prices can be left free to vary, playing their resource-allocating role, while simultaneously compensation is provided to counter the detrimental effects of sudden shifts of demand or supply, and the consequent changes in export revenue.

The third cause of a growing inclination towards compensatory finance instead of commodity agreements has been an increasing recognition that the problem experienced by u-countries is not so much that of unstable commodity markets as of unstable and insufficient total export revenue to carry through a program of economic development. Compensatory finance measures are much more suited for this broader stabilization aim.

VII. 2   A comparison with commodity agreements

Export restrictions, multilateral contracts and buffer stocks are all measures which, in order to achieve their specific aim, directly affect a commodity market. In contrast, compensatory finance measures, while they may have the same objectives, are intended to operate outside, or perhaps rather above the commodity market. Let us look in somewhat greater detail at the significance of this difference.

Suppose that the objective pursued is to increase the revenue of the exporting countries during a short period when this revenue, due to a negative shift in demand, has fallen below its trend value. This is illustrated in Figure VII.1, where D_2 is the decreased world demand. As a result of the demand shift, the unregulated export revenue will fall from P_2Q_4 to P_1Q_3.

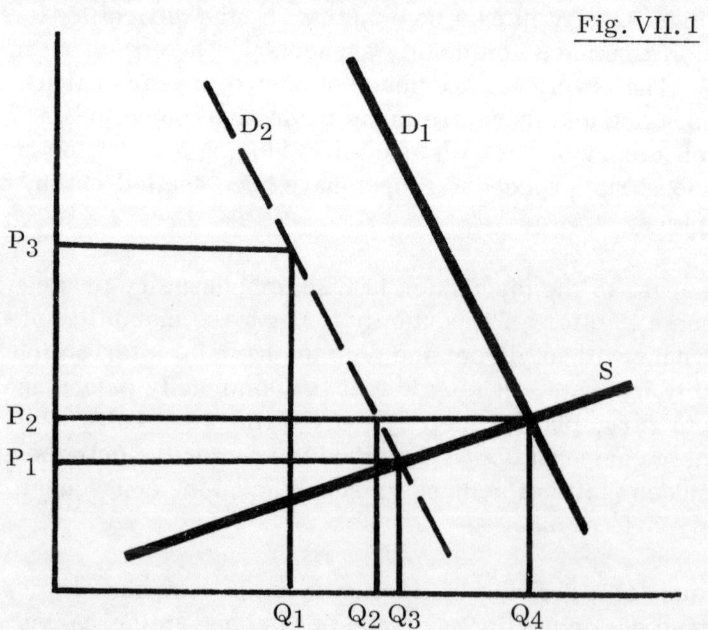

Fig. VII. 1

An export restriction to maintain the revenue of the exporting side will have to decrease the quantity supplied to Q_1, to obtain price P_3, because $P_2Q_4 = P_3Q_1$. The repercussions on the functioning of the market will be important. As a result of the reduction in quantity traded, adjustments have to take place on both the exporting and importing side. If, instead, a buffer stock is used to maintain the earnings of the producing side, prices and quantities traded will be maintained through the additional demand in the shape of purchases by the buffer. For revenue to be maintained at the P_2Q_4 level, the buffer acquisitions will have to amount to Q_4Q_2. The effects on the market due to a multilateral contract scheme will depend on the specific framework of that scheme.

Irrespective of which of the three methods is used, there will be direct effects on the market. Prices will be prevented from falling below their level prior to the demand decrease. In the case of export restrictions, production has to be cut, or alternatively stocks will build up in the exporting countries, while use will diminish or stocks will be consumed on the importing side. If production is not regulated by decree, price maintenance will have an effect on resource allocation. The temporary price fall to P_1 might have led to some move of productive resources away from the commodity concerned. Commodity agreements will preclude any such tendencies. The negative demand shift would result in a decrease of demand to Q_3 in the unregulated market. If price is to be maintained or raised, the quantity demanded from sources other than the buffer stock will be smaller still.

The results of the introduction of a compensatory finance scheme are said to be quite different. For the sake of illustration, and anticipating the classification which follows in the next section, let us discuss here the effects of a specific compensatory finance scheme, the aim of which is to even out the export proceeds from a specific commodity, in comparison with what has been said above on commodity agreement tools.

In principle the compensatory finance measures will in no way prevent the quantity traded from falling to Q_3, and the price from decreasing to P_1. Just as in the unregulated market, revenue will decline to P_1Q_3 as a result of the negative demand shift. The function of the scheme will now be to compensate the exporting countries in part or in full for this fall, e.g. for the difference between P_2Q_4 and $P Q$. The market apparently functions undisturbed. Simulta-

110

neously the temporary fluctuation in export proceeds is evened out
through the compensation payments.

In practice, the government of the exporting country, being the
recipient of compensation, is likely to try to influence the exported
quantity so as to derive the maximum benefit from the compensatory
finance scheme. In the case analyzed here, it would be profitable
for each individual exporting country to diminish export sales as far
as possible, so long as total falls of export revenue from earlier
levels are compensated. Generally applied, such national policies
will of course render the scheme politically untenable, because
those who pay compensation would hardly be willing to contribute to
cover a decrease in export revenue caused by a deliberate policy on
the part of exporting country to diminish the quantity of exports.
The problems encountered in this connection will be further discussed in the following sections of this chapter.

VII.3 <u>Classification of compensatory finance scheme proposals</u>

No less than ten major proposals for compensatory finance have
appeared since 1953. [3)] Some of them resemble commodity agreements by attempting to stabilize the trade conditions of particular
commodities only, while others attack the problem at a deeper level
by trying to stabilize total export proceeds of u-countries. Of the
various proposals, only one, the IMF-scheme, has been put to a
practical test. It may be instructive at this stage to classify the
proposals each according to its main distinct feature. Thereafter
an attempt will be made to analyze their implications.

In the <u>specific commodity compensatory schemes</u> it is initially
necessary to reach an agreement between the exporter and importer
side on what should be considered as "normal" price, and in some
cases also "normal" volume of exports of the commodity in question,
the deviations from which are to be compensated.

In one of the types within this category, suitably called a "price
compensation scheme", the compensation is based exclusively on
the deviations of unit price from what has been agreed as "normal",
multiplied by the actual export quantity. A slightly different type
among the specific commodity schemes takes volume deviations
from "normal" along with the price deviations as the basis for compensation. Thus, if "normal" export quantity and unit price are 100
and $10 respectively, and if in a particular year - due, say, to a

world depression - only 70 are exported at $6 per unit, compensation will be based on the price deviation, $4, times the "normal" quantity, viz. 100, or $400. The most far-reaching of the specific commodity schemes has as its aim to even out total export proceeds from the commodity in question. Thus again, assuming that the agreed "normal" quantity and unit price are 100 and $10, and that the total "normal" export proceeds consequently amount to $1,000, compensation will be based on deviations of export proceeds from this figure.

In the general compensation schemes, attention is shifted from individual commodity markets to the total export proceeds, or in some cases to the terms of trade of a country. It is the fluctuation of these values which is taken as a basis for compensation.

Other major differing features among the proposals which have been put forward are those of automaticity versus discretion, insurance fund versus ad hoc payments, credits versus grants, and beneficial versus strictly commercial terms applied.

In the automatic schemes, compensation payments should be made as soon as the country's export proceeds decline in accordance with rules that have been specified in advance. This simplifies the procedure, and creates clarity on what to expect for the country which suffers from export instability. As the value of exports can to a large extent be determined by national governmental measures, automatic schemes invite governments to manipulate exports so as to benefit from compensation. This is why, in some of the schemes, payment is discretionary, and made dependent on a scrutiny by the administering body of whether the export shortfall has been "outside the country's control".

Some of the proposals contain rules for the creation by contributions from the participating countries of a fund from which compensatory payments are made. The existence of a fund makes a scheme more firmly established and reliable, particularly in periods of political uncertainty. Other proposals suggest ad hoc payments from the importing to the exporting countries which participate, or vice versa. This ensures a closer contact between the partners in the scheme. In both cases the exporting side is to receive compensation when the price or value in exports falls below the agreed level, while it is envisaged that the importing side be compensated in the opposite case.

There have been a few proposals about compensation on a grant
basis. In view of the vast amounts involved, most cases deal with
compensation in the form of credits. A complicated problem then
arises as to the terms of repayment of credits received. Usually
credits should be repaid within 3-5 years, in periods when export
receipts exceed some kind of agreed average. In one variant of the
1961 UN schemes, [4] dues which the country has not been able to
repay within 3 years are converted into grants.

The terms on which u-countries can participate differ according to
the various schemes. In a few of them, all contributions are to be
made by those nations which will take advantage of compensation
payments. Most proposals, however, postulate that rich countries
should carry a larger burden than poor ones, so that the scheme
becomes beneficial to u-countries. Thus, it may be stipulated that
the initial fund should be created by contributions predominantly
from i-countries, [5] or, when payments are made directly between
the partners, that compensation to the importing countries should
be more limited than vice versa. [6]

VII.4 Effects of compensatory finance measures

Our experience of international commodity agreements has been
fairly thorough, albeit not very encouraging. Not so with compensatory finance. The only scheme put to the test so far has been that
of the IMF, inaugurated in 1963. [7] This scheme is intended to
dampen the fluctuations in the proceeds of merchandise exports, by
allowing special drawings of up to 25% of a member country's quota.
Compensatory drawings are allowed if the country's export proceeds decrease in comparison with the weighted average of exports
in the current and in the two preceding years. In addition, the IMF
must convince itself that the shortfall is "outside the country's
control" and of a temporary nature. Repayment is expected within
a period of 3-5 years.

On a recommendation from UNCTAD I, the IMF in 1966 widened the
credit limit from 25 to 50% of a country's quota. Towards the end
of 1967, one of the documents to UNCTAD II contained the following
somewhat disillusioned passage:

> "So far, however, relatively few countries have availed them-
> selves of this new compensatory facility. This may have been

because relatively few developing countries have qualified for compensatory finance under the IMF rules, or because they have in practice preferred to use their normal drawing rights."[8]

Our analysis of compensatory finance will therefore have to be based in the main on considerations untested in practice.

On theoretical grounds compensatory finance schemes appear to be superior to commodity agreements. Their rules can easily be framed so that there is a minimum of interference in commodity markets. Prices will consequently not be prevented from playing their allocative role. Costs can be kept at a minimum by providing compensation in the form of loans. General compensatory measures seem to be preferable to specific ones. This is because most of the proposals contain some kind of open or hidden assistance feature. Compensatory finance is then used for transfers of resources from i- to u-countries. If the production and export sales of a particular commodity are connected with beneficial compensatory payments, the government of the country, to which compensatory payments accrue, will find it remunerative to encourage or at least to maintain production of the commodity, even if the factors of production could be more efficiently used elsewhere.[9] In the end the result may be a burdensome overproduction, which will be difficult to rectify. General compensatory finance schemes avoid this difficulty. At the national level the problem is the variation of total exchange earned rather than the export revenue from a specific commodity. A stable and reliable exchange supply appears to grow more important as national development planning becomes widespread in u-countries. This again suggests the advantages of compensatory finance over commodity agreements and the superiority of general over specific compensatory measures.
An ambiguity not yet satisfactorily solved remains even with the most general of the compensatory measures. The exchange instability depends not only on a country's exports, but on capital transactions as well. The latter consist of many differing items, which can even out or sharpen the fluctuations of export proceeds. It is reasonable, but very difficult to take capital movements into consideration in compensatory finance schemes. A long-term loan can be a good substitute for exchange earned through exports. This a short commercial credit could hardly be. The way in which different capital inflows and outflows should be treated is a matter of discretion. Strangely enough, this problem is not dealt with at all

114

in the compensatory finance schemes. None of them extends its
definition of instability beyond what is included in export proceeds.
A further complication in the stabilization of exchange availability
arises from the capital flight from u- to i-countries. Very little is
known about the size or stability of this flow. A third difficulty has
been taken up by Clark Reynolds. In a study of Chile, [10] he
analyzes the difference between export proceeds and exchange availability for an economy whose exports are dominated by foreign-
owned companies. In such an economy, according to Reynolds, the
relevant quantity to be stabilized is the "returned value", defined as
total current local payments by the foreign-owned sector, e.g.
wages, domestic purchases for consumption, stock building and
construction, and all taxes. In view of investment cycles and variations in profit repatriation, the exchange availability in a country
like Chile may not necessarily be correlated with exports, and
attempts to even out variations of export proceeds might in fact
destabilize exchange availability.

Fleming's testing

In 1963, a detailed test[11] was undertaken within the IMF of the
Organization of American States Compensatory finance scheme, [12]
which first appeared in 1962, and was intended to cover the Latin
American countries. Under this scheme, a revolving fund would be
established by contributions of $1,200 million from i-countries and
$600 million from u-countries participating in the scheme. The
fund would be used for compensating two-thirds of any shortfall of
export proceeds for u-countries below the average in the previous
three years, in accordance with a formula where deviations of x_t,
the actual export revenue from $\bar{x}_t = \frac{1}{3} (x_{t-1} + x_{t-2} + x_{t-3})$, would
be the basis for compensation. The loans would be subject to a
maximum of 20% of a country's total yearly exports, and repayment
was envisaged within the following five years, irrespective of the
subsequent development of the country's export proceeds.

Fleming starts out by defining the instability of export proceeds as
the deviation of the actual year's proceeds, x_t, from an ideal norm,
$\bar{x}_t$. The ideal norm is based on a five-year moving average, with
year t in the middle. In symbols, instability equals

$$\frac{1}{\bar{x}_t} (x_t - \bar{x}_t), \text{ where } \bar{x}_t = 0.2(x_{t-2} + x_{t-1} + x_t + x_{t+1} + x_{t+2}).$$

In practice, this ideal norm is of little value. One would have to wait for two years before any judgment could be passed on the instability experienced in a particular year. Retrospectively, it gives a good basis for the calculation of export fluctuations. This ideal norm is used for estimating a target level of exchange earnings. Fleming assumes that variations in actual exports will also change import needs. In consequence, only two-thirds of the export deviations from the ideal norm need to be compensated to reach the target level of exchange earnings.

The test consists in measuring for a number of past years the extent to which the availabilities of exchange under the OAS scheme would have corresponded better or worse to the target level than they did in the absence of any scheme. The test was undertaken not only for the OAS scheme, but for a great number of variations from the OAS rules, concerning:

1. Value of parameters and number of variables in the OAS regression from which export shortfalls and compensatory payments are to be calculated.
2. Maximum amount of permitted indebtedness.
3. Provisions regarding repayment.

Only international aggregates were calculated. Individual country studies would obviously have given better insights into the functioning of the schemes. The conclusions are not very encouraging. The improvement of the exchange availabilities relative to the target level through the schemes is very small. Some of the schemes even result in a deterioration of stability as compared with the earnings from actual exports. In the best of the 137 schemes considered, only 23% of the actual deviations from the target level would have been cut out. The original OAS scheme would have given an improvement of only 8%. Schemes in which current year export estimates carry a heavy weight in the regression from which instability is calculated generally give better results. The reason for this is that, in any formula for determining a compensation norm on the basis of past and current data only, considerable weight has to be given to the current year's exports if that norm is to approximate as closely as possible to a moving average centered on the current year.

Somewhat better results are also obtained by cutting out years with rising exports, when in any case the schemes would not have allowed any borrowing. The maximum possible improvement then rises to 38%. Borrowing maxima are estimated for the various schemes. They vary between $590 and $2,770 million. No positive correlation is found between the efficiency of a scheme and its credit requirements.

The disappointing results seem to stem mainly from two causes. One is that repayments in these schemes have to be made irrespective of the further developments of export revenue. If, at the time of repayment, export revenue experiences a new fall below trend, the repayment obligation will in fact act as a destabilizer. The second reason is the inability so far to devise a suitable formula for an automatic compensatory finance scheme. More generally, the problem is to determine the trend value of export revenue for a year without being able to see into the future. And if we don't know the trend value, it is impossible to calculate the degree of current instability. In these circumstances there is a risk that compensatory payments are made at wrong points of time and amount to sums which, viewed retrospectively, will not stabilize the export revenue. An additional difficulty is that there are many differing ways of calculating the trend, and the results obtained may be different from each other.

Even if these difficulties are disregarded we should not forget that what is measured is only the fluctuations of exchange earnings from exports, while no consideration is given to capital movements or to the effects of the foreign-dominated export sector, where it exists, as spelled out by Reynolds. It may very well be that something quite different from export proceeds needs to be stabilized in order to improve the ability of u-countries to carry through their development plans.

By its estimate of credit needs, Fleming's study also directs attention to the necessity to calculate costs, and, in the final evaluation, to compare the costs with the improvements achieved by its operation. This aspect is notably absent from most of the compensatory financial proposals.

The IBRD proposals for supplementary financial measures

Despite the limited use made of the IMF compensatory facility and the disappointing conclusions of Fleming's investigation, a proposal for a new scheme was put forward by the British and Swedish delegates to UNCTAD I. The IBRD was requested to work out the details which were to be further considered by a group of experts, whose recommendations would be taken up at UNCTAD II at New Delhi in 1968. It is instructive to study the objections raised to this scheme, because they are indicative of some general weaknesses of compensatory finance.

The IBRD-scheme[13] belongs to the general discretionary compensation category, which avoids the norm estimation difficulty by stipulating compensation of export shortfalls from "reasonable expectations". The purpose of the scheme is to promote planning and execution of development programs in u-countries which are members. Along with the administering agency, a member country is supposed to draw up a realistic development plan of 4-5 years' duration, which will include estimates of export proceeds and import needs. Any long-term deficiency of exchange to carry the plan through will have to be covered from other sources. The IBRD scheme will only assist with "short-term unexpected shortfalls" of exports. The condition for compensation is that the country has adhered to the jointly agreed development program, so that the export shortfall is really "outside the country's control". In each case before compensation is paid, the agency will be allowed to undertake the checks required to establish the case for compensation, and to determine, in consultation with the country concerned, the amount to be paid out. The proposal is not specific as to the terms of compensation payments. This is left to be determined by the administering agency, although loans on more or less concessionary terms, and grants are both envisaged. On the assumption that compensation from this scheme would be supplementary to credits available from other institutions, like IBRD, IMF, etc., the rough estimate of the need for finance for the first five years, based on a highly simplified simulation exercise, amounts to some $1,500-2,000 million. Most of the money is expected as contributions from i-countries.

Various objections to the scheme were raised by the group of experts,[14] consisting of representatives from fourteen countries, which met late in 1967 to consider the IBRD proposal, and subsequently by the general meeting of UNCTAD II at the beginning of 1968. No final agreement could be reached, and the conference sent the proposal back for reformulation and reconsideration.

118

Apart from objections covering vagueness in several aspects of the
scheme - such as the source and size of contributions, terms on
which compensation would be paid, and the fact that the proposals
contained a duplication of the IMF compensatory financial measures
- two main considerations came out against the scheme. The first
one, voiced primarily by the USA, was the inequitability of the whole
arrangement. The scheme is expected to contain a considerable
amount of assistance, and its purpose is to promote planning and
execution of development programs. The question raised was why
the benefit of this assistance should accrue only to countries with
varying export incomes. Many of those, like for instance Malaysia
or Ghana, are relatively prosperous u-countries, which could afford
on their own to establish the exchange buffers needed to counter
export instability, without too serious internal repercussions. On
the other hand, many very poor countries, like Burma or India,
have fairly stable export earnings, and therefore could not benefit
from the scheme. The constant need in these latter countries
for exchange to carry through their development plans seems to
merit greater sympathy, in view of their poverty. Would it not
therefore be more just to provide more generous support through
IDA, which could allocate it according to genuine needs, rather than
to concentrate assistance on countries with fluctuating exports?
The argument seems valid, and gains strength when the difficulty of
measuring instability is considered. Furthermore, as will be discussed in the next chapter, our knowledge at present of the
detrimental effects of export instability on growth is very meagre.
The effects of compensatory finance assistance on the pace of
development are therefore highly uncertain.

The second major objection to the scheme came from the u-countries
themselves. Supplementary finance was to be provided only to
countries which agreed to draw up a development plan together with
the administering agency, and on condition that the export shortfall
had occurred in spite of the country's adherence to the plan. This
would necessitate considerable powers for the agency to participate
in the long-term decision-making processes, and to scrutinize the
internal affairs of the country concerned. Once it had started to
rely on compensation payments, the country could easily feel that
it had lost some of its freedom of action. In pursuing the aim of the
originally drawn-up plan, the agency might for example find it
necessary to dictate on the use of the compensatory payments. In
fact, the role of the agency could easily develop into something not
dissimilar to that of a supranational treasury, as once recommended

by Tinbergen.[15]   Representatives of several u-countries reacted sharply against this possibility of interference, and their criticism strongly reduced the prospect of reaching a positive decision.

VII.5 Conclusions

Export restrictions and multilateral agreements result in profound and often undesirable repercussions on the commodity markets where they are operated. Buffer stock policies carry heavy costs and require large resources if they are to be operated efficiently. A feature common to commodity agreements in general and to specific compensatory finance schemes is that they even out fluctuations on single commodity markets only. If, therefore, the aim is to stabilize the whole export revenue of primary producing u-countries, general compensatory finance schemes offer a more efficient method. To reach this general aim, a great number of commodity agreements or specific compensation schemes would have to be established, which hardly seems realistic with the post-1945 experience in mind. General compensatory finance offers better possibilities than commodity agreements for avoiding disturbances on the demand or supply side of the commodity markets. This is also one reason for preferring general compensatory finance schemes to specific commodity compensation. Although, ideally, it would be simpler to differentiate between stabilization and assistance aspects, compensatory finance schemes of a beneficial character may be a method of increasing the total amount of aid in a period when the volume of development assistance is stagnating.[16] Much more research is needed into the economic consequences of export instability (see also the following chapter) as well as into the cost of running, and the efficiency of, compensatory finance schemes. The uncertainty surrounding these issues is probably the main reason why u-countries themselves have not yet established an insurance scheme which would guard them against excessive export variations. It seems unwise to spend scarce resources on the very uncertain benefits which might result. It is in view of the great difficulty of establishing a practical and accepted norm for measuring export instability, and of devising formulae whereby an automatic scheme provides a stable exchange flow, that the IBRD has approached the problem by suggesting discretionary measures, directly connected with the receiving country's development plan. Whether, in the final analysis, an international compensatory finance scheme on these lines will be adopted depends much more on political than on economic considerations.

Notes and references to Chapter VII

1) See <u>Kyklos</u>, Vol.XI, 1958, p.141-265 and Vol.XII, 1959, p.271-401.

2) <u>Kyklos</u>, Vol.XI, 1958, p.141-154.

3) See <u>IMF Staff Papers</u>, July 1965, article by G. Lovasy, p.216-221 for a summary description of the various proposals.

4) See International compensation for fluctuations in commodity trade, UN 1961.

5) See for instance Report by the Secretary General to the UNCTAD I, 1964, Chapter III, part A.

6) See UNCTAD I, New York 1964, Proceedings, Vol.III, article by Meade, p.454-455.

7) Compensatory Financing of Export Fluctuations, IMF, Washington, Feb.1963.

8) UNCTAD: Commodity problems and policies, Nov. 67, TD/8, Suppl.1, Stencil, p.53.

9) This point has been brought out by B.Swerling, 'Current Issues in Commodity Policy', <u>Essays in International Finance</u> No.38, Princeton, 1962.

10) Mamalakis and Reynolds, <u>Essays on the Chilean Economy</u>, 1965.

11) Fleming, Romberg, Boissoneault, 'Export Norms and their Role in Compensatory Financing', <u>IMF Staff Papers</u>, March 1963, p.97-146.

12) Final report of the group of Experts on the stabilization of export receipts, OAS, 1962.

13) Supplementary Financial Measures, IBRD, Washington DC, Dec.1965.

14)   See UNCTAD: Supplementary Financial Measures, Final
       Report of the Intergovernmental Group, TD/33, Nov.67,
       Stencil.

15)   See Kyklos, Vol.XII, 1959, p.283-289.

16)   For an elaboration of this argument, see H.G.Johnson,
       Economic Policies towards less Developed Countries, London
       1967, inter alia chapter IV.

VIII THE EMPIRICAL EVIDENCE OF THE EFFECTS OF INSTABILITY

VIII.1 The result of the empirical tests

In chapter II we discussed some of the problems caused by the unstable exports experienced by u-countries. We concluded that these problems must be most serious for countries whose exports contain a very high proportion of commodities, and in particular where the foreign trade is dominated by one or a few commodities only. The same should be valid for countries whose export trade flows mainly towards a particular, limited geographical area. Putting all eggs into the same basket ought to increase the risk of instability. With this background the recommendations offered by economists have been easy to formulate. U-countries should diversify their exports so as to include a greater number of commodities and preferably also a higher proportion of manufactured goods. Furthermore, they should spread their exports to more countries and thereby even out the demand variations likely to occur from time to time in their different export markets.

Not until 1962 were these mainly theoretical considerations confronted with empirical data. In that year, Coppock[1] and Michaely[2] presented the results of their studies, soon followed by Massell in 1964.[3] Finally, in 1966, MacBean's econometric study,[4] which drew freely on the three works just mentioned, was published. Coppock's work is a very broad-based investigation into the dimensions of price, quantity and revenue instability in international trade in general. The book abounds in statistical evidence, and in a sense it forms a basis for the investigations of instability which have been presented since. Michaely has chosen to look into one of the causes of instability, namely commodity concentration in international trade. His interest is directed more towards instability in price, and in the interrelation of the extent of price fluctuations with various aspects of concentration in foreign trade. Massell's article of 1964 tries unsuccessfully to find the explanation of export revenue instability in commodity or geographical concentration of exports.

MacBean, finally, after elaborating on the findings of the other three authors, proceeds a step further in trying to ascertain the effects of export instability on the national economies of u-countries. Some of the findings of these authors have been mentioned in earlier parts of this book. In section I.4, for instance, we discussed Coppock's and Michaely's measurements of relative instability between commodities and manufactured goods.

Although the approach, scope and methodology differ, a number of important conclusions are independently reached by several of the authors. As MacBean's study is the latest, the most penetrating and, in line with the present study, mainly concerned with the problems of u-countries, it has been selected from among the four as the main source of reference in the following discussion.

MacBean finds only an insignificant correlation between export revenue instability and the level of economic development:

> "Once again this (analysis) suggests a tendency for under-
> developed countries to have less stable export earnings.
> But it also suggests that it is a fairly weak tendency, that
> the differences are not large, and that there is a consid-
> erable overlap in experience of instability between rich
> and poor countries."[5]

The three plausible reasons for expecting instability which have been brought up earlier in this section - namely a high proportion of commodities in total exports, dominance of one or a few commodities, and geographical concentration in exports - have, according to MacBean's figures, little value for explaining the instability of revenue which actually exists. The study shows that variable export supply rather than demand has been the important source of price instability. Supply variations, we recall from chapter I, will cause a smaller revenue instability than variations in demand. This may help in explaining MacBean's findings. Supply variations also imply that price stabilization measures might only aggravate revenue instability (see also discussion in section I.5). MacBean's analysis shows that geographical concentration has in fact some stabilizing effect on export revenue. This he explains by the relatively even post-war economic progress of the USA, the UK and France, the dominant importers of commodities.

The apparent implication from these general findings runs counter to the currently accepted policy recommendations. Little would be gained in terms of stability by a country diversifying its exports to a wider geographical area, into a greater number of commodities, or into a larger proportion of manufactures. A point not considered by MacBean is the effect of product diversification on the terms of trade and the total export revenue trend rather than on instability. If a country has been concentrating on commodities with falling price trends, diversification could naturally be of great advantage.

MacBean singles out some ten u-countries which have experienced an especially high degree of instability in their export trade. He finds that in most cases this instability has been peculiar to the country concerned and associated with domestic developments, often with political disturbances, rather than with generally high dependence on commodity trade.

In several attempts, MacBean relates different internal variables to the degree of instability. Among the domestic magnitudes studied in this way are investment, growth of GNP, degree of inflation and availability of reserves. None of these appears to be significantly correlated with export instability, a fact which the author attributes to the operation of built-in stabilizers, in particular to a high marginal propensity to import, the consequent low value of the foreign trade multiplier, and the pattern of distributed lags in reactions to an initial change in export proceeds. The figures emerging from the analysis do not support the common view that instability of export earnings has retarded economic growth in u-countries:

> "The chief conclusion of the first part of the book is that probably the importance of short-term export instability to underdeveloped countries has been exaggerated. There is little evidence to show that in general their economies have been damaged. In most cases fluctuations in income do not appear to be at all closely related to fluctuations in export earnings. Many countries with highly unstable exports have relatively stable incomes. Many with stable exports have serious domestic instability. In few countries is there much sign of strong association, current or lagged, between domestic variables and export fluctuations."[6]

The multiple-country analysis is followed by five individual country studies. The countries have been selected so as to mirror different characteristics of underdeveloped economies, e.g. large versus small, peasant farmer versus large-scale mining production, high versus low geographical concentration of exports and so on. These studies confirm in the main the earlier findings.

In spite of the thoroughness of the study, many lacunae remain. What, for instance, is the inconvenience caused to the economy which has constantly to adapt its imports according to the export revenue fluctuations? What will be the consequences of the necessary import and exchange controls? At one point MacBean notes that u-countries on an average keep higher exchange reserves than i-countries. Is this then a result of their experience of instability? And what is the cost of keeping these high reserves? It is interesting to note the persistent lack of significant correlation between practically all the variables tested by MacBean. As a result, the policy implications which emerge from the analysis are mainly in the negative, indicating what should not be done. Do there simply not exist any important problems generated by general commodity instability? Or could it be that some further analytical work - which will find the important correlations, and can be used for positive policy recommendations - remains to be done?

VIII.2 Implications for commodity stabilization measures

The negative implications for international commodity measures emerging from the empirical studies here referred to, are easy to draw. If we are completely uncertain about the negative effects of instability on the one hand, while stabilization certainly will cost money on the other, then there will be little rationality in establishing commodity schemes. The money needed to operate a scheme could in these circumstances much rather be spent in direct aid programs, whose effects are better known, or alternatively on further research to improve our knowledge of export instability. If, as MacBean concludes, serious and possibly detrimental instability is confined to a few countries, and is due to very special reasons, then it would be more efficient to attack these problems at the national level, close to the source, and to select measures especially suited to counteract the specific conditions at hand, rather than to establish world-wide agreements, the effects of which are widely diffused. The implications also seem to be more against commodity arrangements which carry heavy costs, e.g. buffer stocks or compensatory finance on a grant basis, as compared to export restriction agreements, where the direct costs are negligible.

Could it be that the absence of correlation between export instability and internal disturbances has somehow been intuitively felt by u-country governments, and that this explains why so few commodity agreements have come into operation?

> "MacBean's analysis suggests that, so far as the less developed exporting countries are concerned, this unwillingness (to enter into international agreements) reflects a rational appreciation of the extremely limited value of such insurance in the stabilization of export earnings."[7]

VIII.3 The need for additional research

The main conclusion which emerges is the great uncertainty which surrounds so many of the problems involved. It is relatively easy to analyze theoretically, and with simplifying assumptions, the implications of a particular commodity measure. This has been done in our earlier chapters. But we need to know much more about the underlying causes of the supply and demand behavior in different markets. We need to widen our knowledge of producers' reactions to prices and other variables under varying circumstances, of short- and long-run substitution effects, of interrelationships between commodities, and so on. MacBean's study of the effects of instability is an excellent contribution to the investigation of that particular problem but, as he himself points out,[8] we now require much more detailed research into the domestic consequences of fluctuations, preferably carried out at the national or sub-national level.

A relatively inexpensive way of reducing instability and simultaneously limiting the risks of inefficient resource allocation in the long run, would be to devote much more effort to long-term projections and indicative plans regarding the production and use of various commodities. Work of this type is already done by FAO in connection with many agricultural commodities. Similar studies would certainly be useful also for non-agricultural commodities. To have any effect, the findings of the studies must be properly distributed to those involved in commodity market decisions.

On the basis of the additional knowledge and information emerging from the studies suggested here, it would certainly become much easier both for producers and users to make more rational long-term decisions, which would diminish the fluctuations of the supply and demand schedules. Instability and risks of losses in commodity markets would also thereby be decreased.

The studies would provide the decision-makers in commodity markets with a better grasp of the detrimental effects on the national economy resulting from commodity instability. Simultaneously, proper calculations would become available on the costs of various stabilization measures. If the need for commodity stabilization were still felt, a much firmer ground would be availabl₂ from which to decide on the choice of optimal policy.

Notes and references to Chapter VIII

1)   J.D.Coppock, _International Economic Instability_, New York 1962.

2)   M.Michaely, _Concentration in International Trade_, Amsterdam 1962.

3)   B.F.Massell, 'Export concentration and export earnings', _American Economic Review_, March 1964.

4)   A.MacBean, _Export Instability and Economic Development_, London 1966.

5)   A.MacBean, p.36.

6)   A.MacBean, p.339.

7)   H.G.Johnson, _Economic Policies towards Less Developed Countries_, London 1967, p.144.

8)   A.MacBean, p.341.

BIBLIOGRAPHY OF WORKS CITED

Balassa, Bela, Trade Prospects for Developing Countries, Illinois 1964.

Bentzel, R., Lindbeck, A. & Stahl, I., Bostadsbristen, IUI, Stockholm 1963.

Bohm, P., Pricing of Copper, Stockholm 1966.

Brown, L.R., 'The Agricultural Revolution in Asia, Foreign Affairs, July 1968.

Caine, S., 'Instability of Primary Product Prices', Economic Journal, Sept. 1954.

Cohen-Cyert, Theory of the firm, New Jersey 1965.

Commodity Yearbook, New York, 1964.

Coppock, International Economic Instability, New York 1962.

The Economist, Oct. 14, 1967; Nov. 2, 1968.

FAO, Agricultural Marketing Boards, Rome 1966.

FAO, Commodity Review, Rome, 1966 and 1968.

FAO Monthly Bulletin of agricultural economics and statistics, referred to as FAO Monthly Bulletin, Rome.

Fleming et al., 'Export Norms and their Role in Compensatory Financing', IMF Staff Papers, May 1963.

Grubel, H.G., 'Foreign Exchange Earnings and Price Stabilization Schemes', American Economic Review, June 1964.

Heller, N.W., Fiscal Policies for Underdeveloped Economies, Harward Law School, Cambridge, 1954.

IBRD: Supplementary Financial Measures, Dec. 1965.

IMF: Compensatory Financing of Export Fluctuations, Washington, Febr. 1963.

International Tin Council, Statistical Bulletin, London.

International Tin Council, Statistical Yearbook, London.

IWC, World Wheat Statistics, London, 1966.

Johnson, H.G., Economic Policies Towards Less Developed Countries, London 1967.

Johnson, H.G., 'The Destabilizing Effects of International Commodity Agreements on the Prices of Primary Products', Economic Journal, Sept. 1950.

Keynes, J.M., 'Note on the Return of Estimated Value of Foreign Trade of the UK at Prices of 1900', Economic Journal 1912.

Kyklos, Vol. XI, 1958 and Vol. XII, 1959.

Lerdan, 'Stabilization of the Terms of Trade, Kyklos, Vol. XII 1959.

Lovasy, G., 'Survey and appraisal of proposed schemes for compensatory finance', IMF Staff Papers, July 1965.

Lundberg, E., Problem omkring produktionsfunktionsanalysen, Stockholm 1968.

MacBean, A., Export Instability and Economic Development, London 1966.

Mamalakis and Reynolds, Essays on the Chilean Economy, Homewood, Ill. 1965.

Massell, B.F., 'Export Concentration and Export Earnings, American Economic Review, March 1964.

Michaely, M., Concentration in International Trade, Amsterdam 1962

Myint, H., 'The Classical Theory of International Trade and the Underdeveloped Countries', Economic Journal, June 1958.

Nurkse, R., 'Trade Fluctuations and Buffer Policies of Low Income Countries', Kyklos, Vol.XI, 1958.

Nyberg, L. & Viotti, S., Terms of trade mellan utvecklade länder och utvecklingsländer, Trebetygsuppsats, Handelshögskolan, Stockholm, June 1968.

OAS, Final Report of the Group of Experts on the Stabilization of Export Receipts, 1962.

Pincus, J., Economic Aid and International Cost Sharing, Baltimore 1965.

Pincus, J., Trade, Aid and Development, New York 1967.

Reynolds, C.W., The Mexican Economy. To be published in 1969.

Rowe, J.W.F., Primary Commodities in International Trade, Cambridge 1965.

Scitovsky, T., Welfare and Competition, London 1952.

Snape and Yamey, 'A Diagrammatic Analysis of some Effects of Buffer Fund Stabilization', Oxford Economic Papers, New Series, Vol.15, July 1963.

Swerling, B., 'Current Issues in Commodity Policy', Essays in International Finance, No.38, Princeton 1962.

Tobin, J., 'A Survey of the Theory of Rationing', Econometrica, Oct.1952.

UN Statistical Yearbook.

UN Yearbook of International Trade Statistics.

UN, International Compensation for Fluctuations in Commodity Trade, 1961.

UNCTAD I, UN, New York 1954:
Report by the Secretary General to Unctad
Proceedings, Vol.III, Commodity Trade

UNCTAD II:
Stencilled documentation presented to the conference in New Delhi, India, in February 1968.